I0536529

SELF PUBLISHING IN THE AGE OF AI

A PRACTICAL GUIDE FOR THE MODERN AUTHOR

Dale Nicholson

Copyright © 2025 Dale Nicholson.
All rights reserved.

979-8-9933692-3-5 - hardcover
979-8-9933692-4-2 - softcover
979-8-9933692-5-9 - epub

BISAC Codes: LAN015000, COM087000, REF020000
Thema Codes: AKL, UYQ, CJC, AKLB, VSD

Published by Healing Cross Publishing

HEALING CROSS
PUBLISHING

To every author with a story to tell, this book provides the map.

CONTENTS

Introduction

Your Co~Pilot for Modern Self~Publishing

The world of self-publishing has been revolutionized by technology, and the rise of powerful, accessible Artificial Intelligence is the next great leap forward. This book is not about teaching you how to write a better story. It assumes you have a story to tell. Instead, this book is a practical, hands-on guide to navigating the entire publishing *process*, from a finished manuscript to a published book, using modern tools and AI as your indispensable co-pilot.

We will explore how to leverage AI for brainstorming, research, marketing, and even audiobook production, transforming tasks that once took weeks into work that can be done in an afternoon. This book is designed for two types of authors, the **Strategist** and the **Technologist**, and will provide clear pathways for both. Whether you want to use powerful, user-friendly software to get to market quickly or build a custom, automated publishing system from the ground up, you will find the tools and workflows you need here.

Watch for sections throughout the book with typical methods used by these two roles for accomplishing the tasks discussed in that section. It's not a hard and fast rule for what you should use, but just a general idea of common methods used.

Often the path you follow will depend on your way of working and how deeply you want to dive in to the underlying technology.

How to Read This Book

This book is not designed to be read linearly from front to back. It is a reference manual, a playbook to be consulted as you navigate the different stages of your publishing journey.

The best way to start is to identify your primary mindset. Are you an **Author-Strategist**, focused on results and efficiency, or an **Author-Technologist**, focused on control and customization? Use that lens to dive into the sections that are most relevant to your immediate needs.

Here is a map of the territory:

- **Part 1: Pre-Production** is where every project begins. This section covers the foundational work of refining your story, understanding your audience, and performing the critical legal and ethical checks before you begin production.

- **Part 2: Production & Distribution** is the factory floor. Here we turn your manuscript into a professional product and place it on the world's shelves. This section details the major publishing platforms and provides practical workshops for creating your cover, metadata, and pricing strategy.

- **Part 3: Tools & Resources** is your arsenal. This is a detailed reference guide to the specific software and services—from AI assistants to design programs—that power a modern author's workflow. Consult this section when you need to choose the right tool for the job.

- **Part 4: The AI-Powered Author** is the deep dive. This final, forward-looking section explores the next horizon of AI in publishing, from building a custom writing assistant to creating AI-narrated audiobooks and automated marketing engines.

Why I Wrote This Book

This book began not as a grand project, but as a personal one. My wife had written a beautiful book that had sat unpublished for years, and I had two of my own gathering dust. I started building a system to solve our problem.

My wife, like many others, had no interest in allowing AI to touch her manuscript and we did not do so, but simulating workshops to get better keywords, understanding the formatting requirements for the various publishers, and other publishing related tasks were no problem. Many others have no problem at all with using AI to help articulate the actual text. And finally, there are people everywhere between. I fall somewhere in the middle and for this book I utilized an AI partner for portions of the book, editing, and adapting to my writing "voice". I'm assuming that if you bought this book, you are interested in doing the same. Even if you use AI extensively, I would encourage you to be very meticulous about reading through and editing the book to update things to be closer to your own voice. I think you'll find it's not nearly so easy to have AI "write a book" for you as so many seem to think. Assistance with formatting, sure, research, great, but the themes and driving intelligence have to come from you. Today's writing is being heavily influenced by AI as people stop using m-dashes, stop putting two spaces after periods in sentences, and all kinds of things that I used to commonly do in my writing, with the express goal of not sounding like AI. It's interesting that AI only wrote that way because of the data it was trained on: writing from actual people. Interesting. I can't wait to see where we go next.

As an Enterprise Architect, I design and build systems for a living. I soon realized that the process of publishing a book could be approached with the same logic: a series of defined steps, powered by the right tools, that could transform a creative work into a commercial product, efficiently and professionally.

The more I researched, the more I saw that the old ways of doing things were no longer sufficient. The rise of AI presented a massive opportunity, but also a new layer of complexity. This book is the result of that journey. It is the system I built, the playbook I developed, and the guide I wish I'd had when I started. My hope is that it will empower you to finally get your own story into the hands of readers.

———————————————

1

PART 1: THE PUBLISHING WORKFLOW: YOUR STRATEGIC MAP

Every successful book is the result of a successful system. This section provides the strategic map for that system. It is an overview of the entire self-publishing journey, from raw idea to finished product.

Think of this not as a rigid set of rules, but as a tour of the territory. At each stage, you will make decisions that shape your final book. The path you take will depend on your goals, your budget, and your personal style as an author.

Throughout this guide, we will explore two primary paths:

- The **Author-Strategist** will focus on finding the most efficient, high-impact route, often leveraging best-in-class tools and services to save time.
- The **Author-Technologist** will focus on building a robust, automated system, often using open source tools to gain maximum control and long-term flexibility.

This workflow is your guide to making conscious, informed decisions at every turn. Let's begin, this first section covers the main phases:

THE THREE PHASES OF PUBLISHING

The journey from manuscript to marketplace can be broken down into three core phases:

1. Pre-Production

Goal: To forge your raw manuscript into a professionally polished, market-ready asset. This is where you refine your story, define your audience, and prepare for the technical work ahead.

2. Production

Goal: To transform the polished manuscript into a beautiful, saleable product. This phase covers everything from interior formatting and cover design to generating the final, valid files for ebook and print.

3. Distribution

Goal: To place your finished book onto the digital and physical shelves of the world's largest retailers. This involves choosing your platforms, setting your price, and navigating the final steps to publication.

2

Pre~Production

The Story

If you are reading this book, I suspect you have already written or started writing a book and that you are beginning to think about how you will get it published.

It's perfectly fine to skip this chapter if you feel you're already past this step. However, this chapter exists to remind you that the story is the core product. Whether you are writing fiction or non-fiction, any genre, you have to have a story worth telling if you want people to purchase your book.

No matter how well you master all the other skills related to self-publishing, none of it will matter if the book itself isn't of good quality.

How you get the story into a format fit for publishing can be quite different depending on your own style, preferences, and technical ability.

As mentioned earlier, this book was written to follow two primary paths, and that starts from the very beginning. You might use a completely different way to get your ideas down that someone on the other path. Also, even within the same path there are multiple ways to done, which is why there is an extensive section later in the book outlining the tools available today for each area related to publishing.

The Strategist's Path:

- **Process:** Your focus is on getting the ideas down clearly and structuring the narrative logically. Use tools that feel familiar and don't get in the way of your creative process.
- **Toolset: LibreOffice Writer** is a capable and familiar starting point. For more structured work, purpose-built applications are superior. Don't let not having the "right" tool stop you from capturing your ideas.
- **Recommendations:** Use **Scrivener** for its powerful organizational features. It's available for Mac, Windows, and Iphone/Ipad, if you use more than one operating system you do need to buy separate licenses though. **Manuskript** is an open-source alternative, it's not nearly as polished but can give you a good start if you need to be careful about your budget.

- **Note:** *What's true with both of these solutions is that they don't fully handle the formatting. If you are particular about the formatting you'll need to consider additional tools either that work with these tools. One example is Scrivomatic which is an add on for Scrivener that integrates Pandoc to provide more advanced output formatting capabilities.*

The Technologist's Path:

- **Process:** Your focus is on creating a clean, future-proof source text that separates content from presentation. This allows for maximum automation and control in later stages.
- **Toolset:** Write in a plain text format like **Markdown** using a powerful text editor like **VSCodium** or **Vim** and ensure you initialize a git repository so you can track changes.
- **Recommendations:** The entire project should be managed under version control with **Git**. This provides a complete history of your work and facilitates branching for experimental rewrites.
- **Note:** *As a technologist, you might still enjoy using a tool like Scrivener. I have successfully utilized the windows version of that tool on linux using some extra help which will be covered in more detail later.*

AI-Assisted Path (Content):

- **Brainstorming & World-Building:** Use Gemini or another AI to break writer's block or flesh out ideas. "My fantasy city needs a system of magic. Give me three distinct systems and describe the potential societal impact of each."

PROFESSIONAL EDITING

Why This Matters: This is the single most important signal of quality and respect for the reader. It is a non-negotiable investment in your book's professionalism and your author reputation. This step is universal to both personas.

Self-Editing (Pre-flight Check):

Strategist's Path: Use the built-in tools in **LibreOffice Writer**.

- **Recommendations:** Augment the basic check with a more advanced tool like **ProWritingAid** or **Grammarly**, which integrate directly with LibreOffice Writer.

Technologist's Path: After running a basic spellcheck, use a powerful open-source checker.

- **Recommendations:** Use **LanguageTool** from the command line or within an editor like VSCodium for its robust, offline capabilities.

The Professional / Paid Path (Hiring):

- **Recommendations:** For a debut novel, hiring a **Line Editor** or **Copy Editor** is crucial. Find an editor who specializes in your genre via a curated platform like Reedsy. You are not just buying proofreading; you are buying expertise in reader expectations for your market.

- **Types of Editing:** Developmental (plot), Line (prose), Copy (grammar), Proofreading (final check).

- **Typical Costs:** $0.02 to $0.08 per word, depending on the service.

AI-Assisted Path (Pre-Editing Polish):

- Prompt to help you fix macro-level problems before paying a human editor to find them.

> *"Act as a developmental editor. Read the following chapter and identify any potential pacing issues or unclear character motivations."*

PRE~PRODUCTION IN PRACTICE

Understanding the concepts of pre-production is the first step. The following workshops in this section will guide you through the practical application of these ideas, helping you to define your book's market position and create a plan for its success. The "Blurb Writing Workshop" will help you craft compelling marketing copy, and the "Platform Audit Workshop" will help you devise a strategy to reach your target audience.

3

COMMON STORY STRUCTURES

Understanding the fundamental architecture of storytelling is a crucial part of the pre-production process. While there are endless ways to tell a story, most successful narratives are built upon a handful of time-tested structures. This chapter provides a brief overview of the most common frameworks used by authors today.

THE THREE~ACT STRUCTURE

This is the most fundamental and widely known narrative structure in Western storytelling, dating back to Aristotle. It divides a story into three distinct parts:

- **Act I: The Setup:** The protagonist, their world, and the central conflict are introduced. This act ends with an "inciting incident" that propels the hero into the main story.

- **Act II: The Confrontation:** This is the longest act, where the protagonist faces a series of escalating obstacles and complications in pursuit of their goal. It often contains a "midpoint" reversal of fortune.

- **Act III: The Resolution:** The story's climax occurs, where the protagonist confronts the central conflict head-on. This is followed by the falling action and the final resolution, showing the aftermath and the new state of the protagonist's world.

THE HERO'S JOURNEY (MONOMYTH)

Popularized by Joseph Campbell in his book *The Hero with a Thousand Faces*, this is a more detailed, archetypal pattern that focuses on the transformation of the protagonist. It's a common framework for fantasy, science fiction, and adventure stories. Its stages can be broadly summarized as:

1. **Departure:** The hero receives a "call to adventure," initially refuses it, but is then encouraged by a mentor figure to leave their ordinary world.

2. **Initiation:** The hero crosses the threshold into the unknown world, where they face a series of trials, meet allies and enemies, and approach the "inmost cave" for a central ordeal.

3. **Return:** After surviving the ordeal and seizing a "reward" (a physical object or new knowledge), the hero embarks on the road back, is pursued, and is ultimately resurrected and transformed upon their return to the ordinary world.

Freytag's Pyramid

Developed by 19th-century German novelist Gustav Freytag, this structure analyzes a story in five parts, creating a pyramid or arc shape. It is particularly useful for analyzing dramatic and tragic works.

1. **Exposition:** The introduction of characters, setting, and background information.

2. **Rising Action:** The series of events that build suspense and lead to the climax.

3. **Climax:** The turning point of the story, where the protagonist's fate is decided.

4. **Falling Action:** The events that occur after the climax, as the consequences unfold.

5. **Dénouement (or Resolution):** The final outcome and the tying up of loose ends.

SAVE THE CAT!

This is a modern, highly prescriptive story structure developed by the late screenwriter Blake Snyder and detailed in his influential book, *Save the Cat! The Last Book on Screenwriting You'll Ever Need*. While originally for screenplays, its 15-beat "beat sheet" has been widely adopted by novelists for its clear, plot-driven framework.

It is important to note that "Save the Cat!" is a copyrighted methodology. The following is a descriptive summary, and authors are strongly encouraged to read Snyder's original work for a full understanding. The structure includes key "beats" such as:

- **Opening Image:** A snapshot of the hero's world and problem.

- **Theme Stated:** A line of dialogue that foreshadows the story's central theme.

- **The "Save the Cat" Moment:** A scene where the hero does something likable to win the audience's favor.

- **Catalyst:** The inciting incident.

- **Break into Two:** The moment the hero decides to enter the new world or take on the challenge.

- **Fun and Games:** The "promise of the premise," where the hero explores the new world.

- **Midpoint:** A "false victory" or "false defeat" that raises the stakes.

- **All Is Lost:** The lowest point for the hero.

- **Finale:** The hero uses the lessons learned to resolve the central conflict.

- **Final Image:** A mirror of the opening image, showing how the hero has changed.

Book Design: Crafting the Visual Product

Cover Design

Why This Matters: The cover is your primary marketing tool. It must convey genre and professionalism in a fraction of a second.

The Strategist's Path:

- **Mindset:** Your goal is a professional cover that sells the book, not to become a graphic designer. Your time is better spent on marketing strategy.

- **Recommendations:** Buy a professional cover. This is one of the wisest investments you can make.

  - **Option 1 (Best Value):** Purchase a Pre-made Cover ($75 - $250).

  - **Option 2 (Premium):** Hire a Custom Designer from a platform like Reedsy or 99designs ($500 - $1500+).

  - **Option 3 (Internal):** Commission an Author.

  - **Option 4 (DIY):** Use **Canva** if budget is the absolute primary constraint.

The Technologist's Path:

- **Mindset:** You want full control over the final product and have the skills to execute a professional design.

- **Recommendations:** Use **GIMP** for photo manipulation and layout, **Krita** for digital painting/illustration, and **Inkscape** for all vector work (like typography and logos). This open-source trio provides a complete, professional grade design suite.

- **Process:** Create separate files for your ebook front cover and your full print wrap. Use distributor-provided templates to ensure correct dimensions, resolution (300 DPI), and color profiles (sRGB for KDP, CMYK option for IngramSpark). Version all designs using Git.

AI-Assisted Path (Concepting):

- Use image generation tools for different stages: **Midjourney** for initial creative concepts and **Adobe Firefly** for final, commercially safe assets.

- Example prompt for generating a picture:

> *"cinematic book cover, sci-fi noir, a lone detective in a worn trench coat, seen from a low angle, standing on a rain-slicked street reflecting neon signs from futuristic skyscrapers. Moody, atmospheric lighting. Style of a modern graphic novel. –ar 2:3"*

Interior Formatting (Typesetting)

Why This Matters: Professional formatting provides a seamless, enjoyable reading experience. A bad interior screams "amateur."

The Strategist's Path:

- **Mindset:** You need a beautiful, professional result without a steep technical learning curve.

- **Recommendation: Use a purpose-built application.** The cost of the software is easily offset by the time and frustration saved.

  - **Option 1:** Use **Vellum** (Mac-only) or **Atticus** (cross-platform). You import your document, choose a pre-designed style, and it exports flawless files.

  - **Option 2:** Hire a **professional formatter** ($150 - $500), an excellent choice for complex books.

  - **Option 3:** Commission the **Author-Technologist** to run your manuscript through their production pipeline.

The Technologist's Path:

- **Mindset:** You require absolute control over typography and layout, and you want an automated, repeatable process.

- **Recommended Path:** Implement a **Pandoc + LaTeX** workflow.

  - Write in **Markdown**.

  - Use **Pandoc** as the conversion engine.

  - Use **LaTeX** with a custom template for typesetting. This allows you to define your typographic styles with code.

  - Automate the entire compilation process with a Makefile or shell script.

- **Alternative for Complex Layouts:** For visually complex books (e.g., image-heavy manuals), **Scribus** is the recommended tool.

- **AI-Assisted Path:** Prompts:

> *"**For the Strategist:** Brainstorm five compelling chapter title styles I could look for in a tool like Vellum or Atticus. My book is a historical biography."*

> *"**For the Technologist:** Write a Pandoc command to convert a set of Markdown files (chapter1.md, chapter2.md) into an EPUB3 file. It should use the cover image 'cover.jpg' and include the metadata from 'metadata.yaml'. Add the '–epub-embed-font' flag for all fonts in the 'fonts/' directory."*

TECHNICAL PREPARATIONS: ISBN MANAGEMENT

Why This Matters: Owning your ISBN makes YOU the publisher of record, providing maximum flexibility and control to use your book across any printer or distributor. A "free" ISBN from a platform locks you to that platform. This step is universal and critical for both personas.

Recommendation: Purchase ISBNs in blocks of 10 or 100 from your national provider (e.g., Bowker in the US). Meticulously track their assignment to each book format (ebook, KDP paperback, IngramSpark paperback, etc.) in a spreadsheet. This is a core business asset.

When you buy a ISBNs, Bowker will also attempt to upsell you to buy things like barcodes and QR codes. You do not have to have these, most of the book services you'll use to publish your books will automatically generate the bar codes needed at no cost. IngramSpark puts it right into the cover template when you create the template. KDP inserts it into the blank spot it saved for the ISBN in the templates you generate there when you upload your cover.

You will want to use the same ISBN between every publishing location for a single edition, typically a softcover, hardcover, and an epub. There will be more detail later under the other chapters for each place where you can publish your book. For now, just keep in mind that you'll either need to use an ISBN provided by the printer (e.g. Amazon KDP or whoever), or provide your own. If you use one provided by the printer, you won't be able to use it anywhere else even if you really are using the same size and type of book elsewhere. This can be confusing for distributors looking to purchase your book to place into bookstores as an example.

I recommend that if you expect to publish anywhere other than a single vendor that you buy your own ISBNs. Then use one ISBN for each book type (hardcover, softcover, epub) that you then use for all the platforms. However, if you make your version different, like say 6x9 for IngramSpark and 5x8 for Amazon, you would still need a different ISBN. Things like the dimensions of the physical book are also associated with the ISBN. In my case, I was creating a single 6x9 hardcover version for both Amazon KDP and IngramSpark so I was able to share the same ISBN on both. Later if I put out a new edition I will need to use another ISBN for that even if it's the same size. If you want to save some money and get something released quickly there could still be some benefit with using a service like Amazon KDP to release something using an ISBN provided by them for free, just be aware you can't also release it anywhere else without making a new version with your own ISBN. Amazon KDP doesn't even require you enter an ISBN for ebooks at all and won't assign one unless you also create a print version, just for some additional color.

PRODUCTION IN PRACTICE

Understanding the concepts of production is the first step. The following workshops in this section will guide you through the practical application of these ideas, helping you to make key decisions about your book's final form. The "Cover Design Workshop," "Metadata Workshop," and "Pricing Workshop" will provide you with the tools to create a professional and marketable product.

5

AI and Copyright Sanity Check Workshop

Artificial Intelligence is a revolutionary tool for authors, capable of accelerating everything from brainstorming to marketing. However, this new power comes with new responsibilities. Using AI-generated content without care can introduce legal and ethical risks into your work.

This workshop is not legal advice. It is a practical, risk-reduction checklist. Its goal is to empower you with a clear process for using AI responsibly, allowing you to leverage its power with confidence and integrity.

Understanding the Landscape

To use AI safely, you only need to understand two core concepts:

1. **Ideas vs. Expression:** In copyright law, ideas, facts, and concepts are not protected. The specific *expression* of those ideas is what's protected. The exact words, the specific brushstrokes, that's what is protected. AI is a fantastic tool for generating ideas. The risk emerges when you use its specific *expression* without modification.

2. **Licensed vs. Unlicensed Data:** AI models are trained on vast datasets. Some, like **Adobe Firefly**, are trained on a library of licensed content, and Adobe provides copyright indemnification, meaning they will legally protect you if you use the generated images commercially. Most other models are trained on data scraped from the public internet, which may contain copyrighted material. Using images from these models for a commercial product carries a small but real legal risk.

THE SANITY CHECK CHECKLIST

Before you publish any work created with AI assistance, you must be able to answer "yes" to the following questions.

The "Rewrite and Rephrase" Rule:

- **Question:** Have I significantly rewritten all AI-generated prose in my own, unique voice?

- **Why:** You should never copy and paste large blocks of AI-generated text directly into your manuscript. Use the AI's output as a first draft or a source of ideas, but the final words must be yours. This not only protects you legally but also ensures your book maintains a consistent voice.

The "Verify, Don't Trust" Rule:

- **Question:** Have I independently verified every factual claim or historical detail suggested by the AI?

- **Why:** LLMs are known to "hallucinate" or confidently state incorrect information. You are the final authority for your book. You should check facts against a reputable, primary source.

The "Attribute with Confidence" Rule:

- **Question:** If I am discussing a specific, trademarked, or copyrighted methodology (like "Save the Cat!"), have I clearly cited the original creator and their work?

- **Why:** Summarizing and discussing other people's ideas is fine, but you must give credit. This demonstrates good faith and respects the intellectual property of others.

The "Commercially Safe Image" Rule:

- **Question:** For any AI-generated image that will be used on my cover or in my marketing, was it created with a service that provides commercial indemnification?

- **Why:** Your book cover is a commercial product. To eliminate legal risk, you should only use images from a service like **Adobe Firefly** that is explicitly licensed for commercial use. Use other, more creative models for ideation and inspiration, but not for the final, published asset.

A Practical Workflow

Here is a simple, step-by-step process you can use to audit your finished manuscript before it goes into production.

1. **Isolate AI-Generated Content:** If you used an AI to help draft certain scenes or sections, highlight them.

2. **Perform the Rewrite Pass:** Go through each highlighted section and rewrite it from the ground up. The goal is not to just change a few words, but to re-express the core idea in your own voice.

3. **Fact-Check:** For every factual claim in your book, add a comment in your manuscript with the source you used to verify it. This creates a clear audit trail for yourself.

4. **Check Attributions:** Search your manuscript for any mention of specific, branded concepts or methodologies. Ensure that the original creator is named and their work is cited in the text.

5. **Audit Your Images:** Look at your cover and any marketing images. Confirm that the final versions were generated using a commercially safe, indemnified service.

By making this "Sanity Check" a non-negotiable part of your pre-production process, you can publish your work with the confidence that you have used these powerful new tools both effectively and responsibly.

Blurb Writing Workshop

A book's "blurb" is an important marketing tool for an author. It's the sales display that shows people what your book is about and convinces them to buy. This workshop provides a framework for writing a compelling, effective blurb.

Deconstructing a Great Blurb (15 minutes)

Goal: To understand the core components of a blurb that works.

Activity:

1. **Select a Bestseller:** As a group, pick a well-known, bestselling book in your genre.

2. **Read and Dissect:** Read the book's description aloud.

3. **Identify the Components:** On a whiteboard (physical or digital), identify and label the key parts of the blurb. Look for:

   - **The Hook:** The opening sentence or two designed to grab the reader's attention.
   - **The Character Introduction:** A brief introduction to the protagonist and their world.

- **The Inciting Incident:** The event that kicks off the story and introduces the central conflict.
- **The Stakes:** What the protagonist stands to lose if they fail.
- **The Cliffhanger:** The final sentence that leaves the reader with a burning question, compelling them to find out what happens next.

THE BLURB WRITING FORMULA (30 MINUTES)

Goal: To apply the discovered components to your own book.

Activity:

1. **Use the Formula:** Using the five components identified above as a template, write a first draft of your book's blurb. Don't worry about making it perfect; just get the core ideas down.

   - **Hook:** Start with a question or a bold statement.
   - **Character:** Who is your protagonist and what do they want?
   - **Conflict:** What is the main obstacle standing in their way?
   - **Stakes:** What are the consequences of failure?
   - **Cliffhanger:** End with a question that implies the story's core dilemma.

2. **Peer Review (Think, Pair, Share):**

   - **Think (5 mins):** Read your draft and identify its weakest point.
   - **Pair (10 mins):** Share your blurb with a partner. Give and receive constructive feedback. Is the hook strong? Are the stakes clear?
   - **Share (15 mins):** Each pair shares one key piece of feedback they received that could benefit the whole group.

Polishing and Keywords (15 minutes)

Goal: To refine the language and optimize for discovery.

Activity:

1. **Strengthen Your Verbs:** Go through your draft and replace weak verbs with strong, active ones. (e.g., "He went to the city" becomes "He raced to the city").

2. **Incorporate Keywords:** Weave in 3-5 of the most important keywords you identified in the Metadata Workshop. They should feel natural, not forced.

3. **Read it Aloud:** Read your final blurb aloud. Does it flow well? Is it exciting? This is the best way to catch awkward phrasing.

By the end of this workshop, you will have a powerful, polished blurb that is ready to be deployed on retail sites and in your marketing materials.

An Alternate Approach: AI Simulated Blurb Workshop

You can use an LLM as a tireless copywriter to help you draft and refine your blurb.

The Master Prompt

Provide the AI with your book's core synopsis and ask it to apply the blurb formula.

Example Master Prompt:

"Act as an expert book copywriter. I am providing you with the synopsis for my non-fiction book, 'Self-Publishing in the Age of AI.' Your task is to simulate a blurb writing workshop.

1. **Analyze the Synopsis:** Read the synopsis and identify the core audience and conflict.
2. **Apply the Formula:** Using the five key components (Hook, Character/Audience, Conflict, Stakes, Cliffhanger), write a first draft of a compelling blurb.
3. **Refine and Polish:** Rewrite the draft into a final, polished short description suitable for a book's back cover.
4. **Create a Longer Version:** Write a longer, more detailed version suitable for an Amazon A+ content page, expanding on the key benefits for the reader.

Synopsis: [Paste your book's synopsis here]"

The Simulated Outcome

Running this simulation for this book yielded a much stronger, more market focused blurb.

- **Analysis:** The AI identified the weakness of the original description, noting it lacked a strong hook and clear stakes.
- **The Formula:** It generated new components, framing the "conflict" not just as the publishing process, but as the risk of being "left behind" by technology.
- **The Final Blurb:** It combined these elements into a compelling narrative:

The world of publishing has changed. Are you equipped to succeed, or are you being left behind? For the modern author, success requires more than just a great book—it requires a smart, efficient, and powerful workflow.

"Self-Publishing in the Age of AI" is the definitive guide to navigating the entire publishing process. This book provides a comprehensive playbook for two distinct types of authors: the results-oriented **Strategist** and the control-oriented **Technologist**. Whether you want to use powerful, user-friendly tools to get to market quickly or build a custom, automated publishing empire from the ground up, you will find the clear, actionable steps you need to thrive.

This process transforms a simple description into a powerful piece of marketing copy.

7

DISTRIBUTION, LAUNCH AND MARKETING

Goal: To strategically place your book in the market, make it discoverable, and execute a marketing plan to drive sales.

DISTRIBUTION PLATFORMS AND STRATEGY

Why This Matters: To build a resilient author career, you need to reach readers wherever they are. This requires a strategic combination of platforms to access online retail, physical bookstores, and libraries. The platforms themselves are web-based, so this section is universal. The key difference is the files you prepared in the previous ste

Recommendation (for starting): The Amazon First Strategy. This approach maximizes your visibility on the world's largest bookstore through Kindle Unlimited, which is a powerful discovery engine, while still ensuring your print book is available to bookstores and libraries via IngramSpark. It provides a focused start with the highest potential for initial velocity.

Alternative (for long-term brand building): The Going Wide Strategy. This diversifies your income streams and builds independence from a single retailer. A good goal after establishing a readership.

Platform Overview: The core platforms are detailed later in the book, but the next section provides an overview level for quick comparison.

Core Platform Comparison

This comparison is designed to give you an at-a-glance summary to help you decide which platform to use for each specific format and goal.

———————————————

Amazon Kindle Direct Publishing (KDP)

Pros	Cons
Massive Audience: The largest single bookstore in the world.	**Vendor Lock-in:** KDP Select is an all-or-nothing 90-day commitment for your ebook.
Seamless Integration: Your print & ebook versions are perfectly linked on one product page.	**Lower Print Royalties:** Royalties on print copies are generally lower than IngramSpark.
Kindle Unlimited: Access to a huge pool of subscription readers if you go exclusive.	**Weak Bookstore Distribution:** The "Expanded Distribution" channel is not a viable option for physical bookstores.
User-Friendly: Easiest interface to learn and use.	**Limited Print Options:** Fewer trim sizes, paper types, and no dust jacket hardcovers.
Fast & Cheap Author Copies: Best place to order copies of your own book for personal use or direct sales.	

IngramSpark

Pros	Cons
Unmatched Global Reach: The #1 gateway to 40,000+ bookstores, libraries, and schools worldwide.	**Higher Complexity:** The interface is less intuitive; pricing (wholesale discount, returns) requires decisions.
Professional Credibility: Being in the Ingram catalog signals professionalism to booksellers.	**Stricter File Requirements:** Less forgiving of errors in cover and interior PDF files.
Higher Quality Print: More paper/trim options and superior hardcover choices (e.g., dust jackets).	**Upfront Costs:** A setup fee per title (though often waivable with promo codes).
You are the Publisher: More control over metadata and listing details in the professional ecosystem.	**Slower & Pricier Author Copies:** Not as efficient as KDP for ordering your own books.
Higher Potential Royalty: You control the wholesale discount, allowing for higher per-unit profit on non-Amazon sales.	

DRAFT2DIGITAL (D2D)

Pros	Cons
Go Wide with Ease: Upload once to distribute your ebook to a dozen+ retailers (Apple, Kobo, etc.).	**A Middleman's Cut:** They take ~10% of the royalty from each sale as the price of convenience.
Saves Immense Time: Eliminates the need to create and manage multiple accounts.	**Less Direct Control:** You have less granular control over pricing and promotions on individual stores.
Library Access: The easiest way to get your ebook into library systems like OverDrive and Hoopla.	**Reporting Delays:** Sales reporting can be a month or two behind what you see on KDP.
Helpful Tools: Provides Universal Book Links (UBLs) and automated back-matter.	**Ebook Focused:** Their core strength and primary use case is ebook aggregation, not print.
No Upfront Cost: They only make money when you do.	

Pricing and Metadata

Why This Matters (Rationale): Metadata is how you speak to the store's search algorithm. Good metadata makes you visible; bad metadata makes you invisible. This is a universal strategic task.

Recommended Path:

- **Pricing:** Research the top 20 books in your most specific sub-category. Price your book within the same range. For ebooks, aim for the 70% royalty tier on KDP ($2.99-$9.99).

- **Description (Blurb):** Write compelling sales copy, not a summary. Use the "Hook, Problem, Promise, Final Question" formula.

- **Keywords & Categories:** Use a tool like Publisher Rocket or extensive manual research to find niche, high-traffic keywords and categories where you can realistically compete.

- **AI-Assisted Path:** Use Gemini to brainstorm keywords, categories, and blurb variations.

Example Prompt:

> *"Generate 20 potential Amazon KDP keywords for a cozy mystery book. The main character is a baker, it's set in a small English village, and there's a cat. Think like a reader searching for their next book."*

Marketing and Promotion

Why This Matters (Rationale): A great book with no marketing is a commercial failure. A strong launch drives sales velocity, which algorithms reward with more visibility.

The Foundation (Author Platform):

Strategist's Path:

- **Recommendation:** Use a simple website builder like **Squarespace** or **Wix** and an integrated email service like **ConvertKit**. The goal is a professional-looking site that is easy to maintain and gets you to market quickly.

Technologist's Path:

- **Recommendation:** Build and host your own website using a static site generator like **Hugo** or **Jekyll**. Host it on **Netlify** or **Vercel** for free, automated deployments from a Git repository. Integrate a self-hosted open-source mailing list solution like **Listmonk**. This provides maximum control, performance, and zero cost outside of hosting.

Both Paths:

- **Pre-Launch:** Build buzz with a **Cover Reveal** and gather reviews with **Advance Reader Copies (ARCs)**.

- **Launch Week:** Drive sales with email/social announcements and paid promo newsletters.

- **Post-Launch:** Maintain momentum with **Paid Ads** (Amazon, Facebook) and engage with **Content Marketing**.

Example Prompts:

- **For the Strategist:**

"Write three different versions of a Facebook ad for my new fantasy novel. The first should focus on the main character, the second on the world, and the third on the core conflict. The tone should be epic and exciting."

- **For the Technologist:**

"Create a Python script that uses the Twitter API to automatically post a pre-written promotional tweet from a list at a specified time. Handle authentication and error checking."

Author Platform Audit Workshop

Your author platform is the collection of assets you control that allow you to connect with your readers directly. A strong platform is essential for long term career success. This workshop provides a checklist to audit and improve your platform.

Website Audit (30 minutes)

Goal: To ensure your author website is professional, effective, and serving its core purpose.

Audit Checklist:

- **First Impression (10-Second Test):** Does your homepage clearly and immediately communicate who you are and what genre you write in?

- **Clarity of Navigation:** Is it easy for a visitor to find your books, your bio, and your mailing list signup?

- **Mailing List Signup:** Is your newsletter signup form prominent on the homepage? Is it easy to use? Do you offer a compelling "reader magnet" (a free story, checklist, etc.) to encourage signups?

- **Book Pages:** Does every book have its own dedicated page with a compelling blurb, a high quality cover image, and clear, universal buy links?

- **Mobile Experience:** How does your website look and function on a smartphone? Is it fast and easy to navigate?

- **Author Bio:** Is your "About Me" page up to date? Does it connect with your target reader and establish your brand?

Mailing List Audit (30 minutes)

Goal: To ensure your valuable mailing list is being used effectively.

Audit Checklist:

- **Welcome Sequence:** Do you have an automated welcome email (or series of emails) that new subscribers receive? Does it deliver your reader magnet and set expectations for future emails?

- **Consistent Communication:** Are you emailing your list regularly (but not too often)? A consistent schedule builds reader trust.

- **Content Strategy:** Are your emails providing value beyond just "buy my book"? Consider sharing behind-the-scenes content, recommended reads, or personal updates.

- **Call to Action (CTA):** Does every email have a clear purpose? Whether it's asking readers to buy a book, follow you on social media, or reply to a question, every email should have a goal.

- **List Health:** Are you periodically cleaning your list of inactive subscribers to improve your open rates and deliverability?

Social Media Audit (30 minutes)

Goal: To ensure your social media efforts are focused and effective, not just a time sink.

Audit Checklist:

- **Platform Choice:** Are you on the right platforms for your genre and target audience? (e.g., Booktok/Instagram for YA, Facebook for older audiences, Twitter/X for non-fiction). You do not need to be everywhere.

- **Profile Optimization:** Is your bio on each platform clear and professional? Does it link back to your author website?

- **Content Pillars:** Do you have 2-3 core content "pillars" or themes you post about consistently? This helps build a coherent brand.

- **The 80/20 Rule:** Is at least 80% of your content aimed at providing value, entertainment, or engagement, with only 20% being direct promotion?

- **Engagement:** Are you actively engaging with readers and other authors in your genre? Social media is a two-way conversation.

By regularly auditing these three core components of your platform, you can ensure you are building a powerful and resilient author business.

An Alternate Approach: AI Simulated Platform Planning

For a new book, you can use an AI to simulate this workshop and create a strategic launch plan for your platform.

The Simulation Prompt

Provide an AI with your book's core audience and themes, and ask it to act as your marketing strategist.

Example Prompt:

> *"Act as an author marketing strategist. My new non-fiction book, 'Self-Publishing in the Age of AI,' targets two audiences: non-technical 'Strategists' and tech-savvy 'Technologists.' The book's content is practical and focused on tools and workflows.*
>
> *Your task is to create a platform launch plan:*
>
> 1. ***Platform Choice:*** *Recommend one primary and one secondary social media platform best suited for this book's content and audience. Justify your choices.*
> 2. ***Content Strategy:*** *Define 3-4 content pillars for a blog and/or newsletter that would provide value to this audience.*
> 3. ***Reader Magnet:*** *Propose a compelling, high-value reader magnet to encourage newsletter signups.*
> 4. ***Welcome Sequence:*** *Outline a 3-part automated welcome email sequence for new subscribers."*

The Simulated Outcome

Running this simulation with the updated brief yielded a highly focused and actionable platform strategy that leverages the book's most advanced content.

- **Platform Choice:** The AI recommended a **blog** as the primary plat-form for establishing authority with long-form content, and **X (for-merly Twitter)** as the secondary platform for sharing short, actionable tips and engaging with the writing/tech community.

- **Content Pillars:** It defined clear, high-value content pillars: AI Work-flow Breakdowns (e.g., "How to Create an AI Audiobook Chapter"), Strategist vs. Technologist Case Studies (e.g., "Vellum vs. Pandoc"), and Prompt Engineering for Authors.

- **Reader Magnet:** It proposed a compelling, multi-part reader magnet called **"The AI-Powered Author's Starter Kit,"** containing:

  - A PDF guide: "The 7-Day AI Marketing Plan."

  - A resource list: "5 Master Prompts for Authors" for common tasks like writing blurbs.

  - A bonus template: An SSML (Speech Synthesis Markup Lan-guage) file to give authors a head start on AI audiobook produc-tion.

- **Welcome Sequence:** It outlined a powerful 3-part sequence designed to deliver value and segment the audience:

  1. **Email 1 (Delivery):** Delivers the starter kit and asks the reader to self-identify their interest: "Are you a **Strategist**, a **Technologist**, or an **AI Power-User**?"

  2. **Email 2 (Value):** Provides a quick, actionable tip (e.g., "A 5-minute AI trick for better book blurbs").

  3. **Email 3 (The System):** Connects the small tricks to the book's larger philosophy of building a sustainable author system, fol-lowed by a soft pitch for the book.

This simulation demonstrates how to use AI to quickly generate a sophisticated, targeted marketing plan that leverages a book's most unique and valuable content to attract the ideal audience.

As an interesting side note, despite the results from my simulation, you didn't find my book by reading a blog. I have little interest in spending the time to build a following with a blog, but if I wanted to build a larger reader base it likely would be a great way to do so. You might not want to follow all the advice you get from your simulation or in person workshop and that's perfectly valid. This tool is here to help you get a feel for how to do marketing and turn your book into a business as this is something you have to do yourself when you self publish. If you used a more traditional publisher they would likely be doing much of the marketing for you. I suspect that most people do not have a great feel for how to handle the marketing for their book. In my case, I have enough obligations to my other work that I can't afford the time to manage a blog and will accept that I might not have as many people find my book, but you will need to choose what level of investment you want to make.

Part 2: Production and Distribution

Welcome to the artists studio. This is where your polished manuscript is transformed into a professional product and placed on the digital and physical shelves of the world's retailers.

Choosing your publishing platforms is one of the most critical strategic decisions you will make. It's not just a technical choice; it's a decision about where and how you will meet your readers. Will you grant exclusivity to a single, dominant retailer for maximum visibility, or will you "go wide" to build a more resilient, diversified author business?

This section provides a deep dive into the major players such as Amazon KDP, IngramSpark, and Draft2Digital. It will also cover other key platforms, giving you the data you need to choose the right path for your book.

Production in Practice

Before you can upload your book to these platforms, you must first create the final, production ready assets. The workshops at the end of this section will provide you with the step-by-step, practical guidance to do just that. The "Cover Design Workshop," "Metadata Workshop," and "Pricing Workshop" are essential stops on your journey to publication.

10

AMAZON KINDLE DIRECT PUBLISHING (KDP)

KDP is the publishing portal for the world's largest bookstore. It is a mandatory platform for all self publishers due to its massive audience share. It functions as an integrated retailer, printer, and distributor. Its user friendly interface makes it the easiest entry point for new authors, and its KDP Select program offers powerful promotional tools for authors willing to grant Amazon ebook exclusivity. The exclusivity doesn't have to be in place indefinitely, but runs in 90 day cycles. You could go the first 90 days, then take your book out of that program so you could release on other platforms like Draft 2 Digital that can get you into Nooks and Apple books. The cost is that you loose the extra marketing tools and commission rates get cut in half (from 70% top 35%). Links to the technical specifications and templates are included below, but keep in mind that these are updated regularly, you can find them by searching for the topic if needed.

Links to Official Guides:

- KDP Print Publishing Guide - https://kdp.amazon.com/help/topic/G202169030

- KDP Help Center - https://kdp.amazon.com/en_US/help

- Print Cover Calculator and Template Generator - https://kdp.amazon.com/en_US/cover-calculator Note that the "Cover Creator" is currently part of the book setup workflow.

Interior File Specifications:

- **File Type:** PDF (Recommended), DOCX, KPF. A properly exported PDF is the professional standard. KPF stands for Kindle Package Format and can be created with Amazon's Kind Create tool, it's meant to ensure your book would work on any Kindle device. I had no problems using a pdf generated by my own workflow however, the critical part is to ensure your margins meet the requirements inside your file or Amazon KDP will give you a error when you try to upload the file.

- **Bleed:** Required for any book where images or elements touch the edge of the page. Add 0.125" (3.2 mm) to the outside edges (top, bottom, and side).

- **Margins:** Minimum of 0.25" (6.4 mm) for all inside, outside, top, and bottom margins. Gutter margins (inside edge) depend on page count: from 0.375" for 24-150 pages up to 0.875" for 701-828 pages. These specifications are not something you will have to calculate directly yourself. You will go to your KDP account and use their generator to give you a template that will calculate all of this for you. I use the pdf output template to then import into my graphic program (in my case GIMP, but you might be providing to a designer you hired, or using Photoshop or some other tool instead). The template generator takes the amount of pages, the book size, your ISBN, book type (hardcover/soft), and your binding/paper selections and gives you this template. I do not recommend creating your own from scratch, it's too easy to have a cover rejected that way.

- **Fonts:** All fonts must be fully embedded in the PDF file.

Cover File Specifications:

- **File Type:** A single, print-ready PDF that includes the front cover, back cover, and spine as one image.

- **Resolution:** 300 DPI is the required resolution.

- **Color Profile:** While sRGB is the simplest path, KDP's color conversion has improved significantly. For professionally designed covers, using a calibrated CMYK workflow with the GRACol or SWOP v2 profiles can yield excellent, predictable results. For authors creating their own covers without professional tools, sRGB remains the safest recommendation. In fact, unless you are working with a professional designer familiar with the requirements of Amazon KDP submissions, it can be confusing to navigate what you really need here. As an example, the first time I attempted to publish a pdf I had read the directions provided with the cover template which clearly said I needed a CMYK color profile embedded in my output file, but the reality is that their system cannot even accept that currently, it can only accept RGB that it will then convert using their own CMYK profiles. This was somewhat alarming at first, but hopefully reading this chapter will help you avoid that confusion.

- **Bleed:** A minimum of 0.125" (3.2 mm) of bleed is required on all sides of the cover file. The generated templates will show a pink area around the outsides of the cover to indicate this, it's easy to see what you need to have covered up for bleed while also seeing what will actually be displayed on the cover.

Platform Services:

KDP does not directly offer editing or design services. However, they maintain a directory of vetted third-party providers for tasks like editing, cover design, formatting, and translation.

Link to Service Provider Directory: https://kdp.amazon.com/en_US/help/topic/G201723120

A+ Content:

A significant marketing feature is the ability to add "A+ Content" to your book's product page. This allows authors to create a visually rich description using various modules, including custom images, banners, and detailed text layouts. A+ Content can dramatically improve customer engagement and conversion rates. It is highly recommended to create this content to make your book stand out.

Testimonials & Case Studies:

Testimonial 1 (Author-Strategist Persona): Mark Dawson, a bestselling thriller author, is a major proponent of using KDP Select and Amazon Ads. His case study often focuses on the business and marketing aspects—treating publishing as an enterprise, using ads to drive traffic and sales velocity, and leveraging the Kindle Unlimited page-read income as a steady revenue stream. The focus is on strategy, not technical implementation. Link to Mark Dawson's Self Publishing Formula Courses - https://selfpublishingformula.com/courses/.

Testimonial 2 (Author-Strategist Persona): Lucy Score, a prolific romance author, exemplifies the high-volume publishing model that thrives in KDP Select. Her success is a case study in understanding a target market, rapidly producing books that readers want, and leveraging the visibility of Kindle Unlimited to build a massive following. The focus is on market alignment and production speed. A relevant Publisher's Weekly article discussing her success - https://www.publishersweekly.com/pw/by-topic/authors/profiles/article/91552-lucy-score-s-big-score.html.

11

INGRAMSPARK

IngramSpark is the most important print book distributor for self publishers who want to reach readers beyond Amazon. It is the publisher facing portal for the Ingram Content Group, the largest book wholesaler in the world. Being listed on IngramSpark makes your book available to a global network of over 40,000 retailers, libraries, schools, and online stores. It is the key to getting your book into physical bookstores.

Links to Official Guides:

- IngramSpark File Creation Guide - https://www.ingramspark.com/hubfs/downloads/file-creation-guide.pdf

- Publisher Compensation Guide - https://www.ingramspark.com/guides/publisher-compensation

Interior File Specifications:

- **File Type:** Print-ready PDF/X-1a:2001 is the safest, most widely accepted legacy standard. However, the more modern PDF/X-4 standard is also accepted and offers better handling of transparency and color profiles. For most users, PDF/X-1a is the recommended target to avoid potential issues.

- **Bleed:** A mandatory 0.125" bleed is required on all sides for all files, regardless of whether the interior has bleed.

- **Margins:** A minimum of 0.5" on all outside edges is recommended. Set up your export once to meet these needed interior dimensions and you should have no problems.

- **Fonts:** All fonts must be fully embedded.

Cover File Specifications:

- **File Type:** A single, print-ready PDF/X-1a:2001. Check the settings of your export tools to see what formats you are using. Just like I described for Amazon KDP, for IngramSpark you won't need to manually calculate sizing or bleed for your cover. You will go to your IngramSpark account and use their cover template generator to give you a template. I use the pdf output template to then import into my graphic program (in my case GIMP, but you might be providing to a designer you hired, or using Photoshop or some other tool instead). The template generator takes the amount of pages, the book size, your ISBN, book type (hardcover/soft), and your binding/paper selections and gives you this template. I do not recommend creating your own from scratch. Ingram will generate the ISBN in the template for you. I found it easiest to make a layer cropped just to the ISBN to put above all the other layers of my cover since it's part of the template you won't be rendering for your final cover image.

- **Resolution:** 300 DPI.

- **Color Profile:** CMYK is strongly recommended for predictable color results. All black text should be 100% K (0/0/0/100) only. If you are doing all your own work rather than sending to a professional designer you might not have CMYK options, that's still ok. Be aware the colors might not be exactly what you were seeing on your screen. In my experience, it's very unlikely for this to be a problem unless you were creating an art book or something along those lines.

- **Bleed:** A mandatory 0.125" on all sides. An additional 0.25" "no-fly zone" for text is required around the trim lines. Like with Amazon

KDP IngramSpark provides easy to see color coding in their templates to tell where the bleed area is and where the viewable area is.

Platform Services:

IngramSpark does not offer in-house creative services but recommends authors work with professional designers and formatters. They have a list of "Experts" you can hire.

Link to IngramSpark Experts: https://www.ingramspark.com/experts

Important Considerations:

- **Fees:** IngramSpark traditionally charges fees for file revisions. It is crucial to verify their current fee structure, as this can impact your budget compared to KDP's free revisions. Also, printing costs at IngramSpark tend to be higher than at other providers like KDP, but KDP can't get you into any physical bookstores so it's a tradeoff. Take this into consideration when you are pricing your book, you may want to have the same price on both KDP and IngramSpark, while you might get a bigger commission on KDP. This will allow you to have a single ISBN between the two platforms.

- **Global Connect:** IngramSpark's "Global Connect" program allows your book to be printed in various international markets (e.g., Australia, India, Germany). This can significantly reduce shipping costs and delivery times for international readers, making it a key strategic advantage for authors with a global audience.

Testimonials & Case Studies:

Testimonial 1 (Author-Technologist Persona): In a detailed case study on the Alliance of Independent Authors blog, author Keith Dixon discusses his process of using both KDP and IngramSpark. He details the technical challenges, such as creating two slightly different cover files to meet the different spine width calculations and color profile recommendations, and the strategic benefit of higher per-unit royalties on IngramSpark sales. This highlights the technical precision required to use the platform effectively. Link to the

ALLi Case Study - https://www.allianceindependentauthors.org/case-study-kdp-print-or-ingram-spark/.

Testimonial 2 (Author-Strategist Persona): Orna Ross, founder of the Alliance of Independent Authors, often speaks about IngramSpark from a strategic perspective. The focus is on the importance of "going wide" to create a resilient author business, the necessity of being in the Ingram catalog to be taken seriously by bookstores and libraries, and making smart decisions about wholesale discounts and returns. The advice is about business strategy, not command-line tools. Link to Orna Ross's Author Website - https://ornaross.com/.

12

Draft2Digital (D2D)

Draft2Digital is a comprehensive author services platform. While it began as an ebook aggregator, it has grown to become a primary hub for authors who want to "go wide" with both ebook and print distribution. It is a "one-to-many" service that vastly simplifies the process of reaching dozens of global retailers and library platforms. In 2022, Draft2Digital acquired its largest competitor, Smashwords, solidifying its market position and expanding its distribution network and toolset.

While D2D can distribute to Amazon, most authors publish directly to KDP for better control and use D2D for most other retailers.

D2D is known for its simplicity and flexibility.

Links to Official Guides:

- D2D Support & FAQ - https://www.draft2digital.com/support/
- D2D FAQ Page - https://www.draft2digital.com/faq/

Interior File Specifications:

- **File Type:** A clean, well-formatted DOCX or EPUB file. Unlike print distributors, they do not accept PDFs for ebooks.
- **Formatting:** The key is using paragraph styles correctly (e.g., "Heading 1" for chapter titles) in your source document. D2D's automated conversion process uses these styles to create a clean EPUB.

Cover File Specifications:

- **File Type:** A high-resolution JPEG file.

- **Dimensions:** They recommend at least 1600 pixels wide by 2400 pixels tall.

- **Resolution:** 300 DPI is recommended.

Platform Services:

D2D's core business is its conversion and distribution service, which is free to use (they take a cut of sales).

They also offer several free value added tools, including:

- An automated layout and conversion service that can create a basic but clean EPUB and print PDF from your source file.

- Universal Book Links (UBLs) that provide a single link to your book across all stores.

- Automated author page and back-matter creation.

- **D2D Print:** A full-featured print-on-demand service that provides a direct alternative to KDP Print and IngramSpark. This allows authors to manage their ebook and print distribution from a single dashboard.

- **Payment Splitting:** A highly valuable feature for co-authors and collaborations that allows royalties to be automatically split and paid out to multiple contributors.

- **Expanded Distribution via Smashwords:** The acquisition brought the extensive Smashwords distribution network under the D2D umbrella, including the Smashwords Store and expanded library access.

Testimonials & Case Studies:

Testimonial 1 (Author-Strategist Persona): Author Joanna Penn is a major advocate for "going wide" and often recommends Draft2Digital as the easiest way to do so. Her testimonials focus on the strategic importance of diversifying income streams, reaching international readers on platforms like Kobo, and accessing the library market via OverDrive. The emphasis is on long-term business strategy and saving time. Link to Joanna Penn's resources on selling more books - https://www.thecreativepenn.com/sell-more-books/.

Testimonial 2 (Hybrid Persona): In a post on the popular k-boards author forum, a user details their experience moving from KDP Select to a wide strategy using D2D. They discuss the drop in KU income but the corresponding rise in sales from Apple Books and Kobo, resulting in a more stable, albeit different, income pattern. They praise D2D's simple interface and consolidated sales reporting as a key factor in making the transition manageable. This reflects both a strategic decision and an appreciation for a user-friendly technical solution. (Note: Forum posts are anecdotal, but highly valuable for persona-based insights).

13

Other Publishing Platforms and Channels

Beyond the primary distributors, a healthy ecosystem of specialized platforms allows authors to build their audience and revenue streams in unique ways.

Kickstarter

The premier platform for crowdfunding books. It allows authors to fund ambitious projects (e.g., special editions, audiobooks) and engage their community directly. It's a powerful pre-order and marketing engine, not a long term sales retailer.

For the Author-Strategist: A high effort, high reward tool for launching a new project, especially for authors with an existing fanbase. It allows you to validate demand, raise capital for production, and create a massive launch-day buzz.

For the Author-Technologist: A platform requiring significant project management. The work involves creating a compelling campaign page, managing backer rewards, and integrating the campaign with other marketing tools.

Patreon / Substack

Subscription platforms ideal for authors who want to build a direct, recurring revenue stream. Authors can serialize chapters, offer exclusive content, and foster a close knit community of their most ardent fans.

For the Author-Strategist: The ultimate tool for building a durable author business. It creates a direct financial relationship with your readers, insulating you from the volatility of retail algorithms.

For the Author-Technologist: An API driven content delivery platform. You can automate the process of posting new chapters from your primary manuscript source and integrate the platform with your main author website.

Wattpad / Tapas

Web novel platforms with massive, built in communities, especially for young adults, Romance, and Fantasy genres. They offer a powerful discovery engine and a potential pathway to traditional publishing or media deals.

For the Author-Strategist: A powerful channel for reaching a new, younger audience and building a massive readership before a traditional launch. The focus is on rapid, serialized content and community engagement.

For the Author-Technologist: A content management system for serialized fiction. The technical work involves formatting chapters for the web and managing a high volume posting schedule.

LEANPUB

A unique platform focused on "publishing in progress." It is particularly popular for technical and programming books, allowing authors to release early and often, gathering feedback and earning revenue while they write.

For the Author-Strategist: An excellent choice for non-fiction authors who want to validate their book idea and build an audience as they write. The "variable pricing" model allows readers to choose what they pay, creating a low risk entry point.

For the Author-Technologist: A platform built around a "Book as Code" philosophy. It has first class support for writing in Markdown and integrating with services like GitHub, making it a natural fit for a technologist's workflow.

14

COVER DESIGN WORKSHOP

A structured workshop is an effective way to bridge the gap between an author's vision and a designer's execution, preventing wasted time and ensuring the final cover is both authentic to the book and effective in the market.

This guide outlines a 2-3 hour collaborative workshop process for an author and a designer/publisher to develop a book cover concept.

THE CREATIVE BRIEF

Before any design work begins, a comprehensive **Creative Brief** must be established. This document is the foundation of the entire process, whether you are working with a hired designer or guiding your own work. Its purpose is to translate the abstract ideas of your book into concrete, actionable information. Below are some key questions for your creative brief:

Book Essentials:

Title & Author Name: Exactly as they should appear.

Synopsis: A concise, one-paragraph summary of the plot. What is the core conflict?

Genre & Sub-genre: Be specific (e.g., "Military Sci-Fi," not just "Sci-Fi"). This is the single most important factor for marketability.

The Core Feeling (Publisher-Focused Questions):

Core Themes: List the 3-5 central themes (e.g., "loss," "redemption," "betrayal").

Emotional Tone: What is the primary feeling you want the reader to have when they see the cover? (e.g., "dread," "wonder," "excitement," "comfort").

Pivotal Moment/Object: Is there a single, defining moment, object, or symbol in the book that is central to the story? (e.g., a specific pocket watch, a unique tattoo, a recurring storm).

Market and Audience (Publisher-Focused Questions):

Target Audience: Describe your ideal reader in detail. Age, gender, interests, what other authors do they read?

Comparable Titles: List 3-5 recent (last 2-3 years), successful books in your specific sub-genre. Provide links to their Amazon pages. This is for analyzing current market trends, not for copying.

Visual Preferences:

Visual Likes: What existing book covers do you love (even outside your genre) and why? Please provide images or links.

Visual Dislikes (The 'No' List): Are there any colors, images, or clichés you absolutely want to avoid? (e.g., "no silhouettes," "no cheesy fonts," "no red and black"). This is incredibly important for avoiding wasted work.

_____

WORKSHOP MATERIALS AND ENVIRONMENT

Necessary Materials:

- Large whiteboard or flip chart with markers.
- Sticky notes and pens.
- Laptop with a reliable internet connection.
- Projector or large screen to display websites and images.
- The author's completed questionnaire.
- A selection of physical books (from the designer's collection) that have interesting covers, textures, or typographic treatments.

Setting the Tone:

Start with coffee, tea, or water to create a relaxed, conversational atmosphere.

The designer should frame the session as a "no bad ideas" collaborative exploration. The goal is not to create a final design today, but to agree on a strong *direction*.

Emphasize that the publisher's perspective is to be the "voice of the customer," ensuring the cover works hard in the marketplace.

_____

Workshop Agenda and Structure (2.5 Hours)

Introduction and Goal Setting (15 mins)

If you hired a professional designer, you should expect them to lead the workshop, otherwise you'll step yourself through these.

Stated Goal: "Our goal today is to leave with 1-3 solid, distinct creative directions for the cover that we are all excited about. I will then use these directions to create the first round of mockups."

Briefly review the agenda so the author knows what to expect.

The Story Deep Dive (45 mins)

Purpose: To go beyond the written synopsis and uncover the book's heart.

The designer/publisher asks probing questions based on the questionnaire. For non-fiction, the process is still the same, adjust the questions accordingly for your real world topic.

- "You listed 'betrayal' as a theme. Tell me about the specific moment that theme is most potent."

- "Let's talk about your protagonist. If you had to describe their core emotional journey in three words, what would they be?"

- "When a reader finishes this book, what is the one thing you hope they tell their friend about it? That's the feeling we need to sell on the cover."

- "You mentioned the locket is important. Is it more about the person who gave it to her, or the secret it contains?"

Visual Exploration and Mood Board (45 mins)

Deconstruct the Comps: Project the comparable titles the author provided. Discuss them critically.

- "Notice how all three of these thriller covers use a single, isolated figure and a cold color palette. That's a strong signal to the reader."
- "The typography on this fantasy novel is central to the design. It feels epic and established."

Collaborative Mood Board: Using a tool like Pinterest or a physical whiteboard, start building a visual library for the book.

- Search for images related to the story's themes, setting, and tone.
- Look for color palettes, textures (e.g., old paper, brushed metal), and typographic styles.

Example Prompt: Use Midjourney or DALL-E live in the session.

"Create a photorealistic image of a rusted iron key sitting on a rain-slicked cobblestone street at night, cinematic lighting." Project the results and add the best ones to the board."

Conceptual Brainstorming (30 mins)

Purpose: To translate the abstract mood board into concrete cover ideas.

Word Association: On the whiteboard, write the book's title. Ask the author to list 10-15 words they associate with it. Circle the most visually evocative ones.

Thumbnail Sketching: The designer takes the lead, drawing rough "thumbnail" boxes on the whiteboard. For the DIY designer, even if you aren't great at drawing, still sketch out the ideas as best you can. Those sketches still will help you reenter the context of the moment you drew them.

- "Okay, for **Concept 1: Character-Focused**, let's try a close-up of the protagonist, looking away." (Draws a rough shape).

- "For **Concept 2: Symbolic**, what if we just show the locket, open, with a specific font for the title?" (Draws another box).

- "For **Concept 3: Typographic**, maybe the title is the hero, huge and distressed, with a subtle texture of the forest behind it." (Draws a third).

Using AI to visualize: This is a powerful method for rapid visualization. The best practice is a two-step process:

- **Ideation:** Use a highly creative model like **Midjourney** to generate a wide range of artistic concepts for each of your thumbnail ideas.

- **Production:** Once a concept is chosen, use a commercially safe model like **Adobe Firefly** to generate the final, high-resolution assets that will be used in the actual cover file. This ensures you are protected from potential copyright issues.

Wrap-up and Next Steps (15 mins)

Review the whiteboard. Point to the 1-3 concepts that generated the most energy and excitement.

Summarize the Agreement: "Okay, it sounds like we are all aligned on pursuing Concept 2 (the symbolic approach) and Concept 3 (the typographic approach). I feel confident I can develop some strong options from these."

Outline Next Steps: "My process from here is to spend the next week developing these two ideas into 3-4 initial cover mockups. You will receive those via email by next Friday for your review."

Post~Workshop Actions

Immediate Follow-up: The designer sends a summary email within 24 hours, recapping the agreed-upon creative directions and confirming the timeline.

Design Phase: The designer creates the first round of professional mockups based *only* on the agreed-upon concepts.

Presentation: The mockups are presented to the author with a brief explanation of how each one connects back to the workshop's goals.

————————————————

Project Management and Collaboration Tools

Trello or Asana: Highly recommended for managing the entire process. Create a board with columns for `Creative Brief`, `Workshop Notes & Moodboard`, `Round 1 Concepts`, `Author Feedback`, `Round 2 Revisions`, and `Final Files`.

Miro or Mural: Excellent digital whiteboard tools for conducting the workshop remotely. They are perfect for collaborative mood boards and brainstorming.

Pinterest: The simplest and most accessible tool for building a mood board, especially for the Author-Strategist.

Dropbox or Google Drive: For sharing large design files and final deliverables.

————————————————

Running the Workshop for Yourself

The workshop's structure is a powerful tool for self-discovery, even when you are a team of one. This section outlines how you can simulate the it even if you don't have a team to help you.

You already know the story better than anyone so you skip the **introduction** and **story deep dive** step.

You go directly into the **Visual Exploration & Mood Board** and **Conceptual Brainstorming** steps, with some slight modifications

The Author-Strategist's Path:

Goal: To clarify your own vision and create a detailed brief for a hired designer or to guide your own work in a tool like Canva.

Process:

- **Fill out the Questionnaire:** Do this rigorously. Printing it out and writing by hand can be very effective. This is the most crucial step for you.

- **Build a Mood Board:** Create a secret board on **Pinterest**. Pin book covers you love, color palettes, fonts, and photos that evoke the feeling of your book. Add notes to each pin explaining *why* you chose it.

- **Word Association:** Use a physical notebook or a simple text file to do the word association exercise for yourself.

- **Execute in Canva:** With this clear brief and mood board, you can now search Canva's templates for designs that match your vision, replacing elements and changing fonts with a clear purpose.

- **AI Usage:** You will lean heavily on AI for brainstorming.

Example Prompts:

"Act as my publisher. Based on my synopsis, what are the biggest cover clichés in the cozy mystery genre that I should avoid?"

"Give me five taglines for my book that emphasize the theme of redemption."

Finalizing: At this point you should have your favorite concepts ready. You'll now need to engage a designer, providing them with the concepts. The **Wrap up and next steps** and **Post Workshop Actions** still need to follow.

The Author-Technologist's Path:

Goal: To create a formal design specification and project plan before beginning the technical work in GIMP, Krita, and Inkscape.

Process:

- **Create a Project Repo:** Initialize a **Git** repository for the cover design.

- **The Brief as README.md:** The Creative Brief Questionnaire becomes the README.md file for your project. You will fill it out in Markdown.

- **Mood Board & Assets:** Mood board images, font files, and textures are saved in a structured assets/ directory within the repo.

- **The Workshop as a Design Doc:** Your "workshop" is the process of creating a DESIGN_SPEC.md file. This document will detail the outcomes of your self-interrogation. It will list the chosen color palette (with hex codes), the specific fonts you've selected, and detailed descriptions of the 2-3 concepts you plan to execute.

- **Execute in GIMP/Krita:** You will now create `.xcf` or `.kra` files for each concept, working to match your design spec. Each major iteration is a new commit in Git, allowing you to track your progress and revert if needed.

- **AI Usage:** You will use AI for technical and research-oriented tasks.

Example prompts:

> "What are the standard trim sizes for a mass-market paperback? Provide them in inches." or "Give me a GIMP workflow for creating a non-destructive vignette layer to darken the edges of my cover."

> "Suggest five high-quality, open-source serif fonts from Google Fonts that are highly readable and have a classic feel."

Wrap up and next steps: You'll want to ensure you block some time to do the same steps that a hired designer would have done. Make a point of doing this work as soon as possible as the details will fade very quickly.

Post Workshop Actions: Since you didn't hire a designer, you have to write the designer summary yourself and save it with your book project files or notebook. Capture your mockups the same way and don't forget to document the explanations around what you were thinking when you made them to help you recall later.

An Alternate Approach: AI Simulated Cover Workshop

Instead of working with a human designer, you can simulate the entire workshop process by using a powerful Large Language Model (LLM) as your creative partner. This allows you to move from a vague idea to concrete, visual concepts in a single session.

The following is an anonymized and improved example based on a real-world simulation, demonstrating how to guide an AI through this process for your own book.

The Simulation Prompt (The Briefing)

The first step is to provide the AI with all the necessary context. You will feed it your completed Creative Brief and ask it to act as your creative director.

Prompt example:

"Act as an expert creative director and AI prompt engineer. I am providing you with the complete Creative Brief for my upcoming non-fiction book. Your task is to simulate our Cover Design Workshop.

1. **Analyze the Brief:** Read and understand the core themes, audience, and visual preferences.
2. **Brainstorm Concepts:** Based on your analysis, develop three distinct, high-level cover concepts. Each concept should target a specific emotional or intellectual entry point for the reader. For each concept, give it a name (e.g., "The Mended Heart," "The Blueprint").
3. **Write Initial Prompts:** For each of the three concepts, write a detailed, professional-grade prompt for an AI image generator (like Midjourney or DALL-E) to create the core visual artwork. Explain the rationale behind your word choices in the prompt.
4. **Write Mockup Prompts:** For each concept, write a second, more advanced prompt designed to generate a full front-cover *mockup*, including placeholder typography for the title and author.

5. **Provide a Strategic Analysis:** Conclude with an "Architect's View" that explains the strategic value of each concept and why it would appeal to the target market.

[Paste Your Entire Completed Creative Brief Here]"

Interpreting the AI's Output

The AI will return a detailed response that gives you three fully-formed creative directions. For a book on healing, the concepts might be:

1. **Concept 1: The Mended Heart (Symbolic):** A direct, emotional concept using the Japanese art of Kintsugi (mending broken pottery with gold) as a metaphor for healing.

2. **Concept 2: Resilient Growth (Metaphoric):** A more subtle concept showing a delicate plant growing through a crack in stone, symbolizing hope in a harsh environment.

3. **Concept 3: An Abstract of Gentle Light (Typographic):** A minimalist, modern concept focusing on color, texture, and a powerful title treatment to evoke a feeling of peace.

For each concept, the AI will provide you with the exact, detailed prompts you need to generate the artwork and mockups.

Generating and Refining the Assets

You will now take the prompts provided by the AI and use them in your image generator of choice.

1. **Generate Core Art:** Use the initial, art-focused prompts to generate a wide variety of visual options for each concept.

2. **Generate Mockups:** Use the mockup-focused prompts to see how the concepts look with text. This helps you quickly validate a compositional direction.

3. **Finalize with a Commercially Safe Tool:** Once you have chosen a final direction, use the two-step process (Ideation -> Production) outlined earlier. Recreate your chosen concept using a tool like **Adobe Firefly** to generate the final, legally-safe assets for your cover.

Why This Process Works

Simulating the workshop with an AI is a powerful strategy for the modern author. It forces you to clarify your own vision through the creation of the Creative Brief. It then leverages the AI's speed and breadth to explore multiple creative directions simultaneously, complete with the expert language needed to generate high-quality results.

This process de-risks your creative choices. Instead of committing to a single idea, you can visualize three complete, professional level concepts in minutes. You move into the final design phase with a clear, validated blueprint, saving you countless hours of guesswork and revision. This is the essence of the "Strategist" and "Technologist" mindset combined: a structured, efficient system for producing high quality creative work.

Even if you fully generate your cover, keep in mind that text almost always will need to be added in a tool like gimp or by a hired professional even if you get the art looking just like you want it. You can simulate that too, but there are a whole host of issues when you go to print that are much more easily addressed if you add layers for your text components in a tool like gimp. I recommend you simulate with text, then when you have a prompt generating what you like, remove the text elements and just generate the cover art component, then bring that in to gimp to add layers for the text.

15

METADATA WORKSHOP

This guide provides a step-by-step framework to gather and understand appropriate metadata to ensure your book is found by the right audience.

PRE~WORKSHOP PREPARATION: SETTING THE STAGE FOR SUCCESS

This phase involves equipping authors with foundational knowledge and gathering the right information. Later in this chapter there is a crucial helper to walk you through how to utilize an AI to simulate the workshop. This is very helpful for busy people that might not have a full crew of friends able to help them through this process. I will still walk through the process first to establish the "personas" of the roles that would be needed to do this workshop with real people and to show how you could manually simulate the workshop, if you don't want to use an AI helper. The output of either method will be dependant on your own ability to think through these things, so I highly recommend the mental exercise to ensure you get your book placed properly in online or physical stores.

Note that even though the workshop focuses on some very specific outcomes, not every platform will match up exactly to accept every BISAC code, keyword, or some of the other outputs that we will identify in the workshop. This can be irritating, but it is understandable since each bookseller, printer, etc. has their own processes and methods. This workshop is designed to give you the full detail you would need for the major self-publishing vendors like IngramSpark, Amazon KDP, Draft 2 Digital, and Bowkers. As a specific example, Amazon KDP doesn't have every BISAC code set up in their system, so you might not find an exact match for the codes you identify in the workshop. IngramSpark has a human review for the codes, you don't get to choose them there directly yourself, but can submit recommendations. Different amounts of keywords might be able to be added on one platform, while fewer on another, etc. This is fine, you'll have what you need for any platform.

Publisher Preparation:

As a self-publisher, you have to play all the parts. This first section outlines what a publisher might request of you as an author prior to a workshop. Capture the information directly to use in later steps.

Welcome & Objectives: A brief welcome note explaining the workshop's purpose: to collaboratively define and refine the key discovery elements for their book.

The "Why" of Metadata: A concise, one-page document explaining what book metadata is and why it's crucial for discoverability and sales. Use an analogy like, "Metadata is the digital equivalent of your book's cover, spine, and back cover copy, working to attract readers online." If you don't know this yourself at this point, hang in there, you'll learn what it means as we go through the workshop.

"Know Your Book" Questionnaire: A thought-provoking questionnaire to get authors thinking critically about their work. Sample questions:

- In one sentence, what is your book about?

- Who is the ideal reader for your book? Be as specific as possible.

- What problem does your book solve, or what need does it fulfill for the reader?

- What are three to five key themes or topics in your book?

- List five to ten words or short phrases you think a reader might use to search for a book like yours.

Competitor Snapshot: Identify 2-3 books you see as direct competitors to your new book. Be prepared to discuss what you admire or dislike about these competitors' titles, covers, and descriptions.

Facilitator Preparation:

If you are doing this on your own, again, you will also play the part of facilitator, do the preparation yourself and capture the information directly for use in later steps.

Genre and Competitor Analysis: Take the information gathered in the Publisher Preparation above, and for each book, conduct a preliminary analysis. Look at bestselling books in the genre. What trends do you notice in titles, subtitles, and cover design? What keywords seem to be prevalent? Tools like Google Keyword Planner and Amazon's search bar can provide initial insights.

Familiarize Yourself with BISAC Codes: The Book Industry Study Group (BISG) provides a standardized list of subject categories (BISAC codes) used by the industry to categorize books. While you don't need to be an expert, you should have a basic understanding of the main categories relevant to your books. See the detail section at the end of the workshop plan for a BISAC deep dive. A top three list of BISAC codes is a key deliverable from this workshop.

Prepare Your Presentation: If you were acting as a facilitator you might create a slide deck to guide the workshop, covering the key metadata elements. I am assuming you will be playing all the roles, meaning you'll have to put on your "facilitator" hat to gather the Information needed for the next step of the workshop.

Assemble Your Toolkit: Have a list of helpful online resources ready to share, such as links to the BISAC subject headings list, keyword research tools, and articles on writing compelling book descriptions.

Required Tools and Technologies:

In-Person Workshop:

- Whiteboard or flip chart with markers.

- Sticky notes and pens for each participant.

- Projector and screen for your presentation.

- A "parking lot" space on the whiteboard to jot down off-topic but important ideas to address later.

Virtual Workshop:

- **Video Conferencing:** A reliable platform like Zoom, Google Meet, or Microsoft Teams.

- **Digital Whiteboard:** A collaborative tool like Miro, Mural, or FigJam is essential for interactive exercises. These platforms allow for virtual sticky notes, voting, and real-time collaboration.

- **Shared Document:** A Google Doc or similar for collaborative note-taking and sharing links.

Workshop Agenda and Structure

Use this as a template, but remember to be flexible and adapt to the group's energy and needs if you are conducting the workshop with a real people. To simulate this as an individual, use the information from earlier steps, but this section is difficult to simulate manually by yourself.

You can try to use an AI to for feedback (as described later in this workshop), but it's really best to utilize at least one person from your friend group, several if possible.

Welcome and Icebreaker (15 minutes)

Introduction: Facilitator, briefly introduce yourself and the workshop's goals. Emphasize that this is a collaborative and creative space.

Icebreaker: "Two-Word Book Pitch." Ask the author to describe their book in just two words. This is a fun, quick way to get everyone thinking about the core of their work.

The Power of Metadata (15 minutes)

A brief, engaging presentation on what metadata is and its direct impact on a book's visibility and sales. Use the prepared information from the facilitator preparation.

Explain that good metadata helps their book get discovered by the right readers.

The Core - Title, Subtitle and Description (45 minutes)

Discussion: Start with a group discussion on what makes a title memorable and effective.

Interactive Exercise:

- **Think (5 mins):** Brainstorm alternative titles and subtitles for the book.

- **Pair (10 mins):** In pairs, share ideas and give feedback.

- **Share (10 mins):** Each pair shares one strong title/subtitle combination with the group and explains why it works.

Book Description Deep Dive: Introduce the concept of a "hook" and the importance of a compelling, keyword-rich description.

Group Activity: As a group, workshop the book description. Project it on the screen and have the group offer suggestions for strengthening the opening, incorporating keywords, and clarifying the book's purpose for the reader.

Discoverability: Keywords and Categories (45 minutes)

Keywords Explained Simply: Explain that keywords are the search terms readers use to find books.

Brainstorming Keywords:

- **Individual Brainstorming (10 mins):** Using sticky notes (physical or virtual), authors write down as many potential keywords for their book as they can, one per note. Encourage them to think about characters, settings, themes, and "comp author" (if you liked author X, you'll like this) terms.

- **Group Affinity Mapping (15 mins):** Authors place their sticky notes on the whiteboard. As a group, you will then categorize these keywords into logical groups. This will reveal key themes and potential long-tail keywords.

Introduction to BISAC Codes: Briefly explain what BISAC codes are and their role in placing books on the right "digital shelf." Show them where to find the official list (BISAC are covered in detail later in this section).

Group Exercise: As a group, determine the top 3 BISAC codes for the book. Try utilizing other existing books as examples if there is confusion around BISAC codes. See the BISAC section later in this section for a detailed breakout of how to run this specific group exercise.

The Human Element - Author Bio and Target Audience (30 minutes)

Crafting the Author Bio: Discuss the importance of an author bio that establishes credibility and connects with readers. It should be tailored to the book's genre and audience.

Exercise: "Who is Your Reader?": In small groups, have authors create a detailed "reader persona" for their book. They should give this ideal reader a name, age, interests, and other relevant characteristics. This exercise makes the target audience tangible.

Headshot Discussion: Briefly touch upon the importance of a professional and genre-appropriate author headshot.

Wrap-up and Next Steps (15 minutes)

Review and Q&A: Briefly summarize the key takeaways and open the floor for any remaining questions.

Commitment to Action: Ask the author to share one thing they will do in the next week based on the workshop.

Explain the Follow-up Process: Let the author know what to expect next in terms of receiving the compiled information and finalizing their metadata.

DURING THE WORKSHOP: FACILITATION TECHNIQUES

Assuming you have some friends helping you, keep in mind that your role as a facilitator is to guide, not dictate. Your helpers need to feel comfortable sharing feedback.

Explaining Complex Concepts Simply:

Keyword Research: Frame it as "listening to what readers are asking for." Use simple, relatable analogies. Instead of "search volume," say "how many people are looking for this."

BISAC Codes: Describe them as the "signs in a bookstore that direct you to the right section."

Managing Group Dynamics:

Encourage Participation: Use techniques like "round-robin" sharing where everyone gets a chance to speak. Actively invite quieter participants to share their thoughts.

Stay on Topic: Use a "parking lot" to table discussions that are important but not relevant to the current activity.

Promote Constructive Feedback: Before any feedback exercise, set the ground rule that feedback should be specific and helpful.

Handling Common Challenges:

Resistant to Feedback: Be careful not to get defensive when receiving feedback. Instead ask clarifying questions to understand the perspective. For example, "Help me understand your vision for the title." Often, resistance comes from a place of fear or uncertainty.

Uncertainty: If you struggle to articulate your book's core message, try to describe the book as if you are talking to a close friend. Try to capture the key items you use, that can get you the description you need. The best descriptions typically come from normal conversation.

Dominant Voices: If one person is dominating the conversation, you can politely interject with, "Thank you for that perspective. I'd love to hear what others think as well."

Post~Workshop Activities and Follow~up

The work isn't over when the workshop ends. A strong follow-up process ensures that the momentum and valuable ideas generated are captured and implemented.

Information and Resources to Share (within 24 hours):

Thank You & Summary: Send a follow-up email thanking everyone for their participation.

Compiled Notes: Digitize and share all the brainstormed ideas and notes from the workshop, inviting further comments.

Resource List: Include links to the tools and resources mentioned during the workshop (BISAC list, keyword tools, etc.).

Compiling and Finalizing Metadata:

Draft Metadata Document: Create a new file in your tool of choice for pulling together the strongest ideas for their title, subtitle, description, keywords, and categories from the workshop.

Review and Refine: Review this draft and ask for your participants to review and give feedback. Provide a clear deadline.

Final Version: Incorporate any feedback and share your final version.

Next Steps for Implementation:

Clearly outline your next steps, ensure you utilize the fruit of this labor when you release the book, entering in the appropriate codes when you actually publish.

Consider a three to six-month check-in to see how the metadata is performing and if any updates are needed based on sales data or new reviews.

METADATA COMPONENTS: WHAT ARE BISAC CODES?

Understanding and correctly utilizing these codes is a critical steps in ensuring a book finds its way into the hands of the right readers.

BISAC, which stands for **Book Industry Standards and Communications**, is a standardized system of subject codes used throughout the North American book industry. Think of them as the digital equivalent of the signs in a physical bookstore that direct you to sections like "Mystery," "Cooking," or "Biography."

These nine-character alphanumeric codes are a core piece of a book's metadata, telling retailers, distributors, libraries, and search engines precisely what a book is about. For instance, the code `FIC022020` immediately tells a system that the book is `FICTION / Mystery & Detective / Police Procedural`. This allows for consistent categorization across different platforms, from online giants like Amazon to local library catalogs.

The system is maintained by the Book Industry Study Group (BISG), which regularly updates the list to reflect new trends and topics in publishing. The complete list, which contains over 3,600 distinct terms across more than 50 main subject areas, is available for free on the BISG's website.

Why BISAC Codes are Crucial for Authors

They have a direct impact on a book's discoverability and sales potential.

Physical and Digital Placement: In brick-and-mortar stores, BISAC codes inform booksellers where to shelve a title. Online, they determine the digital "shelves" or categories a book appears in, making it easier for readers to browse and find what they're looking for.

Enhanced Discoverability: The right codes make a book more visible in online searches. A reader searching for a "single parent" book is more likely to find a title correctly coded with "FAMILY & RELATIONSHIPS / Parenting / Single Parent" than one with a more generic code.

Targeted Marketing: Accurate codes ensure that a book is marketed to its intended audience. Placing a book in a niche category can help it stand out and get noticed faster than if it were competing in a highly crowded, general category.

Industry-Wide Communication: BISAC provides a universal language for publishers, distributors, and retailers to communicate a book's subject matter efficiently.

The Process: Choosing the Right Codes in Your Workshop

Best practices recommend selecting up to three BISAC codes for a single title. The first code listed is always considered the most important and should be the most specific and accurate representation of the book.

Brainstorm the Book's Core Identity (10 minutes)

Activity: Ask authors to answer the following questions about their book:

- What is the primary subject of your book? (e.g., a historical romance, a guide to vegan baking, a biography of a scientist).

- Who is your target reader? What sections of a bookstore or categories on a website would they browse?

- Look at 2-3 competing books. What categories do they appear in on-line? (Note: Amazon uses its own category system, but it's often de-rived from BISACs and provides excellent clues).

Navigate the Official BISAC List (15 minutes)

Activity: Direct authors to the **Complete BISAC Subject Headings List** on the BISG website.

1. **Start Broad:** Have them identify the most appropriate top-level category from the 50+ options (e.g., FICTION, BUSINESS & ECONOMICS, JUVENILE FICTION).

2. **Drill Down:** From there, they should click into that main category and find the most specific sub-category that accurately describes their book. The goal is to be as precise as possible. For example, instead of just HEALTH & FITNESS / General, a book about weight loss should use HEALTH & FITNESS / Diet & Nutrition / Weight Loss.

Select and Rank the Top Three Codes (10 minutes)

Activity: Based on their exploration, have each author select the three best codes for their book.

- **The Primary Code:** This must be the *most accurate* and specific code.

- **Secondary and Tertiary Codes:** These can be used to broaden the book's discoverability. For example, a humorous memoir by an astronaut could be categorized under BIOGRAPHY & AUTOBIOGRAPHY / Science & Technology, with secondary codes in HUMOR and SCIENCE / Physics / Astrophysics.

- **Group Discussion:** Have authors share their primary code choice with a small group and explain their reasoning. This peer feedback can be invaluable.

Common Mistakes to Avoid (and How to Address Them)

The "General" Trap: A frequent error is choosing a "General" sub-category when a more specific one is available. For example, using FICTION / Mystery & Detective / General alongside FICTION / Mystery & Detective / Police Procedural is redundant and discouraged. Stress the importance of specificity.

Misrepresenting the Content: Authors should select codes that reflect the entire book, not just a single chapter or minor theme. A book with one chapter on dreams in a non-fiction work does not belong in the fantasy genre.

Mixing Fiction and Non-Fiction: A single title should not have both fiction and non-fiction codes.

Ignoring Updates: The BISAC list is updated annually. Encourage authors to ensure their chosen codes are current.

An Alternate Approach: AI Simulated Metadata Workshop

For the solo author, it can be challenging to gain objective feedback. This is where you can leverage a Large Language Model (LLM) as a creative partner to simulate the workshop process. This allows you to pressure test your ideas and get a "publisher's perspective" in minutes.

The following is a real-world example of this simulation, conducted for this very book.

The Briefing Prompt

The first step is to provide the AI with a comprehensive brief. You will give it the completed "Know Your Book" questionnaire and ask it to act as your publishing expert.

Prompt Example:

> "Act as an expert publisher and metadata specialist. I am providing you with the complete Creative Brief for my upcoming non-fiction book. Your task is to simulate our Metadata Workshop.
>
> 1. **Analyze the Brief:** Read and understand the core themes, audience, and unique selling proposition.
> 2. **Initial Brainstorm:** Based on the brief, generate a list of 10-15 initial keywords. Also, suggest a primary, secondary, and tertiary BISAC code for the book.
> 3. **Publisher's Perspective:** Critically analyze this initial brainstorm. What is weak? What is missing? What is the book's single biggest differentiator that the metadata *must* capture?
> 4. **Final Refinement:** Based on your own critique, provide a final, production-ready list of 7-10 optimized

keywords, 3 final BISAC codes with your reasoning, and 5 final Thema codes with your reasoning.

[Paste Your Entire Completed 'Know Your Book' Questionnaire Here]"

Running the Simulation and Analyzing the Output

For this book, the AI simulation produced the following key insights:

- **Initial Keywords:** The first list was too generic (e.g., "self-publishing").

- **Initial Categories:** The first attempt at categories was inaccurate, failing to capture the crucial "Artificial Intelligence" angle.

- **The Publisher's Insight:** The AI's "Publisher's Perspective" correctly identified that the book's unique selling proposition is the **dual-path approach for "Strategists" and "Technologists."** This insight is the key to effective metadata.

- **Final Metadata:** The AI then generated a much stronger, refined list based on this core insight.

The Validated Outcome

This iterative process resulted in a final, production ready set of metadata that is far more powerful and targeted than the initial brainstorm.

Final, Production-Ready Keywords (12):

1. `AI for authors` (High-level, essential)

2. `AI audiobook creation` (Specific, high-value benefit)

3. `self-publishing guide 2025` (Targets users looking for current info)

4. `book as code` (Niche, but captures the technologist spirit perfectly)

5. `user-friendly publishing tools` (Appeals to strategists)

6. `RAG for writers` (Specific, advanced AI technique)

7. `prompt engineering for authors` (Key skill, high interest)

8. `indie author business` (Focuses on the professional aspect)

9. `custom AI writing assistant` (Highlights a major benefit of Part 4)

10. `automated publishing workflow` (Appeals to the systems-thinking author)

11. `ebook formatting` (Captures the strategist tool users)

12. `generative AI for fiction` (Broader term to catch related searches)

Final BISAC Codes (with reasoning):

1. `LAN015000` - **LANGUAGE ARTS & DISCIPLINES / Publishing**: This remains the correct primary category. It's where the target reader will look first.

2. `COM005060` - **COMPUTERS / Desktop Applications / Word Processing**: This is a more specific and interesting choice than the general AI category. It positions the book as a practical guide for *using* technology for writing and publishing, which is more accurate than being a theoretical AI book.

3. `TEC059000` - **TECHNOLOGY & ENGINEERING / Publishing**: This is a strong third choice that reinforces the technical, systems-based approach of the book, distinguishing it from more general "how to write" guides.

Final Thema Codes (with reasoning):

1. `AKL` - **Publishing industry**: The primary subject. Correct.

2. UYQ - **Artificial intelligence**: The core technology. Correct.

3. CJC - **Writing guides**: The book's purpose. Correct.

4. AKLB - **Self-publishing**: The specific niche. Correct.

5. VSD - **Audiobook production**: A new and crucial addition to reflect the content of Part 4.

This simulation demonstrates that by treating an AI as a collaborator and using a structured, iterative process, you can produce professional grade metadata that will significantly improve your book's discoverability.

16

PRICING WORKSHOP

This workshop steps you through the process to determine the right pricing for your book.

PRE~WORKSHOP DATA COLLECTION

Complete this data collection *before* the workshop. The accuracy of the workshop's output depends on the quality of this preparatory data.

Fixed Production Costs (Total Investment):

- ☐ Professional Editing (Developmental, Line, Copyediting): $_____
- ☐ Proofreading: $_____
- ☐ Cover Design: $_____
- ☐ Interior Formatting (Ebook & Print): $_____
- ☐ ISBN Purchase: $_____
- ☐ Marketing Setup Costs (e.g., website, initial ad spend): $_____
- ☐ **Total Fixed Costs: $_____**

Variable Per-Unit Costs (By Format):

Paperback:

- ☐ Print Cost Per Unit (from KDP, IngramSpark, etc.): $_____
- ☐ Page Count: _____

Hardcover:

☐ Print Cost Per Unit: $_____
☐ Page Count: _____

Ebook:

☐ Delivery Fee Per Unit (if applicable, e.g., KDP charges ~$0.15/MB for sales at 70% royalty): $_____

Competitor Pricing Analysis

Identify 3-5 recent (published in the last 1-2 years) and successful books in your specific sub-genre. For each title, find and record the following data points from a primary online retailer (e.g., Amazon.com):

- **Competitor Title 1:** _____
  - Ebook Price: $_____
  - Paperback Price: $_____ (and page count: _____)
  - Hardcover Price: $_____ (and page count: _____)

- **Competitor Title 2:** _____
  - Ebook Price: $_____
  - Paperback Price: $_____ (and page count: _____)
  - Hardcover Price: $_____ (and page count: _____)

- **Competitor Title 3:** _____
  - Ebook Price: $_____
  - Paperback Price: $_____ (and page count: _____)
  - Hardcover Price: $_____ (and page count: _____)

_____

WORKSHOP AGENDA AND STRUCTURE (2 HOURS)

Objective: To move from raw data to a strategic pricing model for each book format.

The Breakeven Point (30 minutes)

Purpose: Determine the number of copies that must be sold to recoup all initial fixed costs. This is the baseline for profitability.

Formula: `Total Fixed Costs / (Retail Price - Variable Costs - Retailer Cut) = Units to Break Even`

Action Item:

- Facilitator explains each component of the formula using an example.

- Calculate your breakeven point using a *target* retail price for your primary format (e.g., paperback). Acknowledge this is an estimate that will be refined.

Competitor Market Analysis (30 minutes)

Purpose: To establish a data-backed price range for the book's genre, preventing under- or over-pricing.

Process:

- Plot the collected competitor prices on a shared whiteboard or digital space.

- Calculate the **average price** for each format (Ebook, Paperback, Hardcover).

- Identify the **highest** and **lowest** price points for each format.

- Establish the **Market Price Floor** (the lowest viable price) and **Market Price Ceiling** (the highest justifiable price).

- **Decision Point:** Where does your book fit within this range? Consider factors like author reputation, cover quality, and book length relative to competitors.

95

The Pricing Formulas - By Format (45 minutes)

Purpose: To set a specific, profitable list price for each book format.

Ebook Pricing Decision-Tree:

- **Goal:** Maximum Readership/Reach (e.g., first in series)?

  - **Strategy:** Price at the lower end of the market range, often **$2.99 - $4.99**. This also aligns with the **70% royalty tier** on platforms like KDP (for prices between $2.99 and $9.99).

- **Goal:** Maximum Profit/Prestige (e.g., niche non-fiction, established author)?

  - **Strategy:** Price at the higher end, **$7.99 - $9.99**.

- **Goal:** Perma-free or promotional (lead magnet)?

  - **Strategy:** Price at **$0.00** or **$0.99** (typically yields a **35% royalty**).

Paperback Pricing Formula:

- **Formula:** `List Price = (Print Cost Per Unit / (1 - Retailer Percentage)) + Desired Royalty Per Unit`

- **Variable Definitions:**

  - **Print Cost Per Unit:** Your "at cost" price from the printer.

  - **Retailer Percentage:** The portion of the list price the retailer keeps (e.g., 40% for Amazon KDP, 55% for IngramSpark standard wholesale). This is **0.40** or **0.55** in the formula.

  - **Desired Royalty Per Unit:** The dollar amount you want to earn on each sale.

- **Action Item:** Calculate your paperback list price using this formula.

Hardcover Pricing Calculation:

- Use the same formula as the paperback, but adjust for two factors:

    1. **Higher Print Cost:** Input the specific hardcover print cost.
    2. **Higher Perceived Value:** The "Desired Royalty" can be increased to reflect the premium format. A standard hardcover `Value-Add` is often 25-40% higher than the paperback list price.

Launch vs. Long-Term Strategy (15 minutes)

Purpose: To create a dynamic pricing plan.

Launch Strategy Checklist:

- ☐ **Launch Price:** Will you launch at a discounted price for a limited time (e.g., $0.99 ebook for the first week) to spur initial sales and reviews?
- ☐ **Full Price:** Or will you launch at the final, full price to establish value from day one?
- ☐ **Pre-Order Strategy:** Is a pre-order price set?

Long-Term Price Adjustment Plan:

- **Review Triggers:** Schedule a pricing review based on a set timeline or event.

    - ☐ 3 months post-launch
    - ☐ Upon winning an award
    - ☐ Before running a major promotion
    - ☐ Before launching the next book in the series

CORE PRICING CONCEPTS/REFERENCES

Fixed vs. Variable Costs

Definition: Fixed Costs are one-time expenses incurred regardless of how many books are sold (e.g., cover design). **Variable Costs** are expenses incurred on a per-unit basis (e.g., printing).

Pricing Impact: Fixed costs determine the breakeven point. Variable costs determine the minimum price at which a book can be sold without losing money on that single sale.

Royalty Structures (KDP, IngramSpark)

Definition: The formula used by a retailer/distributor to calculate author earnings from a sale. Example: `(List Price x Royalty Rate) - Print Cost = Author Royalty`.

Pricing Impact: You must know the royalty rate (e.g., 60% on KDP for paperbacks, 70% or 35% for ebooks) to accurately calculate your net profit and set a list price that achieves your earning goals.

Perceived Value and Reader Psychology

Definition: A reader's subjective assessment of a book's worth, influenced by cover design, author reputation, page count, and genre.

Pricing Impact: A price ending in .99 is perceived as significantly cheaper than the next whole dollar. A very low price can signal low quality, while a high price can signal authority and expertise. Your price must align with the value you are signaling.

Genre Conventions

Definition: The expected price ranges for a given category of book (e.g., epic fantasy paperbacks are typically longer and more expensive than short romance ebooks).

Pricing Impact: Deviating too far from genre conventions can create friction for potential buyers. Your competitor analysis should reveal these conventions. Pricing outside of them must be a deliberate, strategic choice.

POST~WORKSHOP DELIVERABLE

The final output is a one-page Pricing Strategy Sheet.

Structure of the Pricing Strategy Sheet:

Book Title: _____

Total Fixed Costs: $_____

Market Analysis Summary:

- Genre: _____
- Market Price Floor (Paperback): $_____
- Market Price Ceiling (Paperback): $_____

Final Pricing by Format:

- **Ebook:**

    – List Price: $_____
    – Royalty Rate: _____%
    – Estimated Royalty Per Unit: $_____

- **Paperback:**

  - List Price: $_____
  - Print Cost: $_____
  - Estimated Royalty Per Unit: $_____

- **Hardcover:**

  - List Price: $_____
  - Print Cost: $_____
  - Estimated Royalty Per Unit: $_____

Breakeven Analysis:

- Number of units to sell to recoup Fixed Costs (based on primary format): _____ units.

Launch & Long-Term Strategy:

- Launch Price: $_____ for _____ days.
- Price Review Date 1: _____
- Price Review Date 2: _____

An Alternate Approach: AI Simulated Pricing Workshop

For a solo author, especially one with a digital-first book, you can simulate this entire workshop with an AI to arrive at a data-driven pricing strategy.

The Pricing Prompt

Provide an AI with the data you've collected.

Prompt Example:

> "Act as a book publishing strategist. I am providing you
> with the data for my non-fiction book, 'Self-Publishing in
> the Age of AI.' Your task is to simulate a pricing workshop.
>
> 1. **Analyze the Data:** My fixed costs are $0. My main
>   competitors are priced between $7.99-$12.99 for
>   ebooks and $16.99-$24.99 for paperbacks.
> 2. **Determine Strategy:** My goal is to position the book
>   as a premium, high value resource.
> 3. **Recommend Prices:** Based on the data and strategy,
>   recommend a specific, final price for the ebook and pa-
>   perback editions. Justify your reasoning based on mar-
>   ket positioning and perceived value.
> 4. **Define Launch Plan:** Recommend a launch strategy
>   (discounted or full price) and explain why."

The Simulated Outcome

Running this simulation for this book yielded a clear, premium pricing strategy.

- **Analysis:** The AI noted that with $0 fixed costs, every sale is profitable,
  so the pricing should be based on market position and perceived value,
  not cost plus. It identified the market could support a premium price.

- **Ebook Price: $9.99.** This positions the book at the top of the standard
  market range, signals high value, and maximizes the royalty rate on
  KDP.

- **Paperback Price: $19.99**. This aligns with the upper middle of the competitor range, reinforcing its status as a comprehensive guide.

- **Launch Strategy:** Launch at full price. The AI reasoned that a discount would signal a lack of confidence and undermine the book's positioning as an authoritative resource.

By using an AI as a strategic partner, you can quickly move from raw data to a confident, market-aware pricing model for your own book.

17

PART 3: TOOLS AND RESOURCES

This section is the arsenal for your self publishing journey. It provides detailed information on the specific tools mentioned throughout this book, but more importantly, it offers a framework for choosing the *right* tool for *you*.

The most critical concept to embrace is the distinction between two author archetypes: the **Strategist** and the **Technologist**.

- The **Author-Strategist** prioritizes speed, efficiency, and return on investment. They prefer to use powerful, user friendly tools that abstract away technical complexity, or to hire experts for specialized tasks. Their goal is to get a professional product to market quickly.

- The **Author-Technologist** prioritizes control, customization, and long term scalability. They prefer open source, scriptable tools that give them full ownership of their data and workflow. Their goal is to build a robust, automated publishing system.

Neither path is "better". They are different mindsets. As you read through this section, don't just look at what a tool *does*. Ask yourself which archetype it serves. Understanding your own inclination is the key to building a toolchain that you will actually use and enjoy.

Categories:

- Writing and Organization

- Scrivener
- Manuskript
- Plottr
- Quoll Writer
- Obsidian
- Dendron
- Trelby (screenwriting tool)
- Sudowrite
- Google Drive

- Editing and Word-processing

  - ProWritingAid
  - Grammarly
  - LanguageTool
  - Google Docs
  - Microsoft Word
  - Autocrit

- Design

  - Canva
  - Diagrams as Code: PlantUML, Mermaid, Graphviz & Ditaa
  - Google AI Studio App Builder
  - Boxshot
  - Adobe InDesign
  - Affinity Publisher
  - GIMP (GNU Image Manipulation Program)
  - Inkscape
  - Krita
  - Book Brush

- Publishing Tools

  - Vellum
  - Atticus
  - Scribus
  - Pandoc

- LaTeX
- ElevenLabs
- Audacity
- PWA (Progressive Web App)

- Platform and Marketing

  - Squarespace
  - Wix
  - Hugo
  - Jekyll
  - Hugging Face Spaces
  - Deepsite
  - Mailchimp
  - ConvertKit
  - Listmonk
  - NetGalley
  - Booksirens
  - Booksprout
  - BookBub
  - Publisher Rocket
  - Royal Road
  - BookFunnel
  - StoryOrigin
  - Bookstagram
  - Booktok

- Brainstorm and Collaboration

  - Miro
  - Mural
  - xMind
  - Trello
  - Asana
  - Pinterest

- Adjacent Tools

- Presentations/Slides
  * Cuille
  * Beamer
- Workflow Automation and Integration
  * n8n (pronounced "nodemation")
- Additional Technologist Infrastructure
  * Docker/Devbox Containers
  * Git LFS (Large File Storage)
  * Google NotebookLM

- Others

  - Git
  - Marlowe
  - Context Gem - open source data extraction
  - composio - integration for AI Agents.
  - BargainBooksy
  - Robin Reads
  - Fussy Librarian
  - gradio
  - streamlit

18

WRITING AND ORGANIZATION

*S*CRIVENER

A comprehensive writing studio that combines a word processor with a powerful project management system, allowing writers to organize manuscripts, notes, and research in one place using a "binder" metaphor.

For the Author-Strategist: The premier tool for managing complex, long-form projects. Its strength lies in allowing you to write in non-linear fragments and easily restructure an entire manuscript. This is a one-time purchase that provides an excellent ROI by saving countless hours in organization and revision. While it offers first-class support for Dropbox sync, the latest versions can also sync with other cloud services like Google Drive and OneDrive with some manual setup.

For the Author-Technologist: A self-contained environment for writing. While its proprietary project format is not ideal. Projects are saved as a directory structure with individual files for all your notes and manuscript (rtf files typically). This means you can get at the files even if you don't have a copy of the software on the machine you are on. Unfortunately the UUID keys generated by the system aren't easily duplicated, so that access only helps with read only operations. Even though Dropbox is the supported way to sync between machines, you can take the files and move them any other way you like.

Key Features: Binder interface for chapters/scenes, virtual corkboard and outliner, split-screen viewing of text and research, project and session writing targets, robust "Compile" function for exporting, extensive research management.

Platform Availability: Windows, macOS, iOS. While an official Linux version is not available, the Windows version runs exceptionally well on modern Linux distributions using the latest versions of WINE or Valve's Proton without complex configuration.

MANUSKRIPT

An open-source writing tool with a focus on outlining, organizing, and tracking story elements, inspired by Scrivener.

For the Author-Strategist: A no-cost alternative to Scrivener for those on a tight budget. It provides many of the same core organizational features, such as a hierarchical binder and character management, helping you structure a complex narrative without the financial investment.

For the Author-Technologist: The FOSS (Free and Open Source Software) choice in this category. It's a Qt-based application that fits perfectly into a Linux-centric workflow. While perhaps less polished than its commercial counterparts, its open nature and use of plain text formats for storage make it appealing for those who value transparency and data portability.

Key Features: Hierarchical story structure, character and plot management, distraction-free mode, story object tracking, multiple plain-text export formats.

Platform Availability: Windows, macOS, Linux.

PLOTTR

A visual book planning application that helps authors create and organize timelines, character arcs, and plot points using interactive templates and charts.

For the Author-Strategist: A high-leverage tool for the planning phase. It helps ensure the story structure is sound *before* drafting begins, reducing the need for costly structural revisions later. Ideal for series writers managing complex timelines and character relationships across multiple books.

For the Author-Technologist: An effective database for story logic. It externalizes the plot structure from the manuscript file, allowing for non-linear thinking and easy restructuring. Its ability to export to common formats means it can be the starting point for a more automated drafting workflow, generating Markdown skeletons from the plot data.

Key Features: Visual timeline creation, character arc tracking, plot card organization, series bible creation, export to Word and Scrivener.

Platform Availability: Windows, macOS, iOS, Android, Web.

QUOLL WRITER

A distraction-free writing application designed for creative writers, with features focused on organization and progress tracking, keeping all project-related assets in a single, local, encrypted database.

For the Author-Strategist: A tool designed to optimize the core activity: writing. Its focus on eliminating distractions and tracking writing goals supports consistent output. The integrated character and location management helps maintain consistency, reducing editing time later.

For the Author-Technologist: An interesting local-first, database-driven writing environment. It provides structure without enforcing a cloud-based ecosystem. Its focus on plain text and clear data organization is appealing. The encryption is a notable feature for privacy-conscious authors.

Key Features: Distraction-free writing mode, integrated outline and notes, character/location management, writing timers and goals, encrypted local database.

Platform Availability: Windows, macOS, Linux.

OBSIDIAN

A powerful knowledge base and note-taking application that works on a local folder of plain text Markdown files, emphasizing non-linear thinking through bidirectional linking.

For the Author-Strategist: The ability to link characters, locations, and plot points together creates a searchable, interconnected database of your story world, ensuring consistency across a large body of work.

For the Author-Technologist: The ultimate writing and knowledge management system. Because it operates on a local directory of Markdown files. Its extensibility via plugins allows for the creation of a highly customized build processes and research environments.

Key Features: Bidirectional linking, graph view for visualizing connections, extensive plugin ecosystem, works on local Markdown files, highly customizable.

Platform Availability: Windows, macOS, Linux, iOS, Android.

Prompt Examples:

Strategist: "Create a Markdown template for a character sheet. Include sections for Physical Description, Backstory, Internal Goal, External Goal, Core Conflict, and Relationships with other key characters (with placeholder links like `[[Character A]]`)."

Technologist: "I use Obsidian for my notes. Generate a K-means clustering algorithm in Python to analyze the frontmatter tags in my Markdown files and identify the 5 most common thematic clusters in my writing."

FOAM

An open-source, community driven knowledge management and note taking tool built directly into the VS Code/VSCodium editor. It is inspired by Roam Research and is the spiritual successor to Dendron for many in the VS Code community, but with a more flexible, non-hierarchical approach.

For the Author-Strategist: While still a technical tool, the output of a well organized Foam workspace is an invaluable strategic asset. You will have a hyperlinked, searchable knowledge repository for your book. The strategist defines the *need* for this interconnected knowledge base.

For the Author-Technologist: The ideal choice for those who want a powerful, graph-based knowledge tool that lives entirely within their code editor. Foam leverages the power of Markdown linking and VS Code's existing features to create a highly flexible and extensible system for world building, research, and connecting ideas. It is less rigid than Dendron was, relying on emergent structure.

Key Features: Bidirectional linking, graph visualization of notes, works on local Markdown files, highly extensible via other VS Code extensions, template support for new notes.

Platform Availability: VS Code/VSCodium Extension (Windows, macOS, Linux).

Prompt example:

> **Technologist:** "I'm using Foam in VS Code. Generate a Markdown template for a new character note. It should include frontmatter for `aliases`, `status`, and `faction`. The body should have level-two headings for 'Description', 'History', and 'Relationships', with a placeholder link under Relationships."

TRELBY (SCREENWRITING TOOL)

A free, open-source, and cross-platform screenwriting application focused on providing a simple, distraction-free environment that correctly enforces industry-standard script formatting.

For the Author-Strategist: An author can use Trelby to adapt their novel into a screenplay, creating a new asset that can be pitched. It's a low risk way to explore turning a book into a film or series. It can also be a powerful outlining tool; writing a story in the visual, dialogue heavy screenplay format is an excellent method for testing plot structure and pacing before committing to a full prose manuscript.

For the Author-Technologist: An ideal choice for a writer who values open-source tools and data portability. Trelby uses an open, XML-based file format, making the raw script human readable and exceptionally well-suited for version control with Git. Its native Linux support ensures it can be integrated into any FOSS-based creative pipeline.

Key Features: Enforces correct script format, auto-completion, multiple views (WYSIWYG, draft), robust import/export options (Final Draft FDX, PDF, HTML), character name database.

Platform Availability: Windows, Linux.

SUDOWRITE

An advanced, AI-powered writing environment designed to act as a collaborative partner for fiction authors. As of 2025, it has evolved far beyond a simple brainstorming tool into a full fledged drafting and editing platform.

For the Author-Strategist: This is your AI co-author. Use it to accelerate your entire drafting process. The "Write" feature is no longer simple auto-completion; it can generate entire scenes or chapters based on your outline and character notes. The "Story Bible" feature is now deeply integrated, actively monitoring your manuscript for consistency and providing real time feedback. It's a strategic tool for dramatically increasing production speed while maintaining narrative cohesion.

For the Author-Technologist: An API first narrative engine. The true power lies in using its advanced models programmatically. A technologist can build custom workflows that use Sudowrite to generate first drafts from a Plottr outline, automatically rewrite passages to fit a specific character's voice, or even power an interactive fiction experience for readers.

Key Features: Context aware scene and chapter generation, deeply integrated "Story Bible" for consistency checking, advanced "Rewrite" and "Describe" functions, powerful brainstorming tools, API access for custom integrations.

Platform Availability: Web.

Prompt Example:

Strategist (Prompt within Sudowrite): "Using the attached Story Bible, write a 500-word scene where Elara confronts the antagonist, Lord Malakor, in the throne room. Her goal is to bluff him into revealing his plan. Ensure her dialogue reflects her established cynical but brave personality."

GOOGLE DRIVE

A cloud-based file storage and synchronization service that includes a suite of office applications (Docs, Sheets, Slides).

For the Strategist: The central hub for all business-related documents. It's used to store contracts, final book files, marketing assets, and to collaborate with editors and designers. Its universal accessibility makes it a reliable and simple foundation for a publishing business.

For the Technologist: A simple, scriptable cloud storage backend. Its API allows for files to be uploaded or downloaded as part of an automated workflow (e.g., a script that compiles a book PDF and uploads it to a specific "Final Files" folder on Drive).

Key Features: Cloud file storage and sync, integration with Google Docs/Sheets/Slides, file sharing and permissions controls, accessible from any device.

Platform Availability: Web, Windows, macOS, iOS, Android.

19

EDITING AND WORD PROCESSING

PRO WRITING AID

An AI-powered writing assistant that has evolved beyond a simple grammar checker into a comprehensive editing suite.

For the Author-Strategist: A critical pre-flight check before sending a manuscript to a human editor. Its reports on pacing and sentence variety are valuable, but its true power now lies in its generative AI "Rephrase" feature, which can act as an AI line editor, suggesting ways to rewrite sentences for clarity, tone, and impact. This allows you to perform a significant portion of the line editing process yourself, maximizing the ROI of your professional edit.

For the Author-Technologist: A powerful linter for prose. It provides a suite of data driven analyses that can be used to systematically improve a text. While not a replacement for creative judgment, its ability to flag statistical anomalies (e.g., unusually high adverb usage) provides actionable data points for refinement.

Key Features: 20+ in depth writing reports, real time grammar and style checking, integrations with Scrivener, Word, and browsers, AI-driven sentence suggestions ("Rephrase").

Platform Availability: Windows, macOS, Web, and various application plugins.

Prompt Example:

Strategist: "My ProWritingAid report says my pacing is slow in this chapter [paste chapter]. Analyze the text and suggest five specific areas where I can add more dynamic action, shorten sentences, or increase conflict to improve the pacing."

GRAMMARLY

A cloud based AI writing assistant that has deeply integrated generative AI into its core functionality.

For the Author-Strategist: The ubiquitous tool for ensuring all public facing text is professional and error free. Its generative AI features (GrammarlyGO) now go beyond simple corrections, allowing you to rewrite, summarize, and generate new text for marketing copy, social media posts, and newsletters, significantly speeding up the content creation process.

For the Author-Technologist: A useful, though sometimes intrusive, real time proofreader. Its strength is its accessibility across virtually every platform. While less detailed than ProWritingAid for long form fiction analysis, it is an efficient tool for catching errors in documentation, emails, and commit messages.

Key Features: Real time grammar and spelling checks, tone detector, clarity suggestions, browser and application integrations, generative AI features for rewriting and ideation.

Platform Availability: Web, Windows, macOS, iOS, Android, browser extensions.

Prompt Example:

Strategist (using Grammarly's AI): "Rewrite this book blurb to be more exciting and mysterious, targeting fans of dark academia."

LANGUAGETOOL

An open-source, multilingual grammar, style, and spell checker.

For the Author-Strategist: An excellent, privacy focused alternative to Grammarly, with a strong free tier and support for dozens of languages. It is particularly valuable for authors writing for international audiences or in languages other than English.

For the Author-Technologist: The superior open source choice. It can be self hosted via a Docker container, giving you a powerful, private grammar and style linter that you control completely. This allows for integration into custom editing workflows or scripts without sending your manuscript to a third-party cloud service.

Key Features: Multilingual support (dozens of languages), open-source core, self-hosting option, browser and application add-ons, style and punctuation checks.

Platform Availability: Web, Windows, macOS, iOS, Android, browser extensions, various plugins.

Prompt Example:

Technologist: "Provide a `docker-compose.yml` file to run a self-hosted LanguageTool server, exposing the required port and setting a memory limit of 4GB."

GOOGLE DOCS

A web-based word processor, part of the Google Drive suite, that emphasizes real time collaboration and cloud-based access.

For the Author-Strategist: The go-to tool for collaborative work with editors, alpha/beta readers, or co-authors. Its real-time commenting and suggesting features create an efficient, unparalleled feedback loop. It's the standard for the editorial phase of the project.

For the Author-Technologist: A front-end for collaborative text input. The primary challenge is extracting clean, semantic content. The workflow involves using Docs for collaboration, then using Pandoc to convert the final .docx file into Markdown, stripping out proprietary formatting and creating a clean source for the production pipeline.

Key Features: Real time collaboration, commenting and suggestion modes, extensive revision history, cloud based access from any device, integration with Google Drive.

Platform Availability: Web, iOS, Android.

MICROSOFT WORD

The long-standing industry standard word processor for manuscript submission and professional editing.

For the Author-Strategist: An essential tool of the trade. Even if you draft in another program, you might need Word to interact with editors and formatters, as its "Track Changes" feature is amazing when you are working on editing.

For the Author-Technologist: A legacy output target. It's not a tool for primary creation, but a format that must be produced for collaboration with non-technical partners. The goal is to generate a clean `.docx` file from a Markdown source using Pandoc, preserving comments and footnotes, and then import the edited version back into the plain-text workflow.

Key Features: "Track Changes" feature for editing, robust style and formatting options, universal compatibility in the publishing industry, powerful mail merge features for marketing.

Platform Availability: Windows, macOS, Web, iOS, Android.

Autocrit

An online manuscript editing tool whose key differentiator is that it analyzes your text against a massive database of *actual published, successful novels.*

For the Author-Strategist: This is a powerful data driven editing tool. Instead of generic advice, Autocrit tells you how your manuscript's pacing, dialogue, or word choice compares directly to bestselling books in your specific genre. This provides unique, actionable insights that help you align your book with reader expectations before it ever goes to a human editor, maximizing the ROI of that edit.

For the Author-Technologist: A data driven analysis engine for prose. It functions as a "linter for writers," identifying patterns and potential issues algorithmically. While its suggestions are not absolute, it provides valuable data points that can be used to refine a manuscript systematically.

Key Features: Pacing and momentum analysis, dialogue reports, strong writing indicators (e.g., adverbs, clichés), comparison to bestselling authors, multiple report types.

Platform Availability: Web.

20

Design Tools

Canva

A user friendly, web-based graphic design platform with a focus on templates and ease of use.

For the Author-Strategist: The recommended tool for creating marketing graphics (social media banners, ads, bookmarks) quickly and efficiently. For authors on a strict budget, its cover design templates offer a "good enough" DIY solution.

For the Author-Technologist: While not a tool for granular control, its speed for creating well composed marketing graphics is undeniable. It's a pragmatic choice for tasks where precision and originality are less important than speed and professional appearance.

Key Features: Massive template library, drag-and-drop interface, integrated "Magic" AI features (including Magic Write and Magic Media for image generation, which is powered by commercially safe models), stock photo integration, team collaboration, Brand Kit for consistency.

Platform Availability: Web, Windows, macOS, iOS, Android.

Prompt Example:

>**Strategist (using Canva's Magic Write):** "Generate 5 taglines for a sci-fi novel about a rogue AI who

discovers empathy. The tone should be thrilling and thought-provoking."

Diagrams as Code: PlantUML, Mermaid, Graphviz and Ditaa

A philosophy of creating diagrams by writing plain text descriptions, which are then rendered into images by a compiler.

For the Author-Strategist: Not recommended for direct use. The Strategist would interact with the *output* (the final diagram image) or use a GUI tool like Miro for brainstorming. They would specify *what* diagram is needed and why.

For the Author-Technologist: This is the *only* recommended path for creating diagrams (flowcharts, character maps, sequence diagrams) that need to be versioned and maintained alongside the manuscript. The plain text source files are lightweight, `diff`-friendly for Git, and can be integrated directly into a Pandoc or Hugo build process. Tools like VScodium/VScode have extensions to simplify using them and for previewing them from within markup files. Setup for these tools isn't always obvious, but spending the effort to be able to use them inside a workflow is worth it.

Key Features: Version controllable, plain text source, scriptable generation, ensures consistency, separation of content and presentation.

Platform Availability: These are command-line tools and libraries. They are cross-platform and can be run on any system (Linux, Windows, macOS) with the appropriate runtime (e.g., Java for PlantUML, Node.js for some Mermaid tools).

Prompt Example:

Technologist: "Generate the PlantUML syntax for a sequence diagram showing a user logging into a website. The participants should be User, Web Browser, Server, and Database. Show the steps for entering credentials, POST request, server validation against the database, and returning a success token."

GOOGLE MAKERSUITE / VERTEX AI

A suite of tools from Google that allows users to create simple, shareable, no-code AI applications by grounding a powerful model (like Gemini) in their own data. The "MakerSuite" branding is aimed at individuals and pro-sumers, while "Vertex AI" is the enterprise-grade platform.

For the Author-Strategist: A revolutionary tool for creating unique fan engagement. An author can create an interactive "Ask My Protagonist" app by grounding the model on their series bible. This creates an embeddable *widget* for an author website that transforms it from static to dynamic, offering a unique draw for readers.

For the Author-Technologist: A no-code front-end for Retrieval Augmented Generation (RAG). By grounding the Gemini model on a corpus of data (e.g., world building documents), a technologist can build powerful internal tools, such as a "Lore Consistency Checker" or a character dialogue generator. These apps can also be connected to Google Sheets and other data sources for even more power.

Key Features: No-code/low-code interface, prompt-based application logic, data grounding via file/data source uploads, shareable/embeddable web app links, powered by Google's Gemini models.

Platform Availability: Web.

Prompt Example:

Strategist (Prompt for building the app): "You are Elara, the protagonist from my novel 'Shadow of the Onyx Blade'. You are cynical, witty, but have a hidden heart of gold. You must never reveal spoilers from books 2 or 3. Answer questions from fans based on the provided lore document, always staying in character."

BOXSHOT

A desktop application specializing in creating photorealistic 3D mockups of products, including books, software boxes, and promotional items.

For the Author-Strategist: A professional tool for creating high-quality 3D book covers for marketing. While tools like Book Brush are faster for social media, Boxshot provides superior realism and control for hero images on a website or in a press kit.

For the Author-Technologist: An advanced rendering engine. It offers granular control over lighting, camera angles, shadows, and materials, allowing for the creation of truly custom and photorealistic mockups that stand out from template-based services.

Key Features: Extensive library of 3D shapes, realistic ray-tracing rendering, advanced lighting and camera controls, scriptable for automation.

Platform Availability: Windows, macOS.

Adobe InDesign

The subscription-based, industry standard professional application for page design and layout for print and digital media.

For the Author-Strategist: The tool professional book designers use. The strategy is to hire an expert who uses InDesign rather than incurring the steep learning curve and subscription cost. It is the gold standard for visually complex projects like cookbooks or photo books.

For the Author-Technologist: The definitive tool for achieving absolute control over every typographic and layout detail. Its powerful style sheets, GREP styles, and preflight tools are essential for producing flawless, press-ready files. Its scripting capabilities allow for automation of complex layout tasks.

Key Features: Advanced typography and paragraph styles, robust pre-checking for print validation, deep integration with Adobe Creative Cloud, extensive scripting and plugin support.

Platform Availability: Windows, macOS.

Affinity Publisher

A professional grade desktop publishing application that offers a powerful alternative to Adobe InDesign, available for a one time purchase.

For the Author-Strategist: A highly strategic choice for authors who want professional level design capabilities without a recurring subscription. It significantly lowers the financial barrier to entry, making it a cost effective alternative to outsourcing for the design inclined author.

For the Author-Technologist: A compelling and capable alternative to In-Design. It offers comparable power for most self publishing tasks, including master pages, CMYK support, and PDF/X export. The seamless "StudioLink" integration with Affinity Photo and Designer is a significant workflow efficiency.

Key Features: One time purchase model, StudioLink integration with other Affinity apps, full professional DTP feature set (master pages, text wrapping, print ready export).

Platform Availability: Windows, macOS, iPad.

GIMP (GNU Image Manipulation Program)

A free and open source raster graphics editor for image manipulation, photo retouching, and creating bitmap-based cover art.

For the Author-Strategist: A tool for basic image tasks like cropping an author photo or resizing marketing images. Due to its steep learning curve, Canva is often a more time efficient choice for creating promotional graphics from scratch.

For the Author-Technologist: The essential open-source equivalent to Adobe Photoshop. It is the go to tool for preparing all raster assets. Its scripting capabilities (via Python or Scheme) are a powerful feature for automating repetitive tasks like resizing and applying watermarks to a batch of images.

Key Features: Comprehensive toolset for photo editing and digital painting, extensive plugin support, powerful scripting and automation capabilities, cross platform.

Platform Availability: Windows, macOS, Linux.

Prompt Example:

Technologist: "Write a Python-Fu script for GIMP that takes all .png files in a specified directory, converts them to grayscale, resizes them to 1200px wide, applies a sharpening filter, and exports them as .jpg files at 85% quality."

INKSCAPE

A professional grade, free, and open source vector graphics editor used for creating scalable illustrations, logos, and typographic cover designs.

For the Author-Strategist: Understanding the value of vector assets is key. A strategist would commission a logo or cover title treatment from a designer who might use Inkscape to create an infinitely scalable file that is crucial for professional branding.

For the Author-Technologist: The core tool for creating clean, professional design elements. All typography and non-photographic symbols for a cover should be created in Inkscape to ensure they are sharp at any resolution. Essential for creating assets that look professional in both high-resolution print and on-screen.

Key Features: Full-featured vector editing suite (paths, nodes, shapes), robust typography tools, standards-compliant SVG file format, cross-platform.

Platform Availability: Windows, macOS, Linux.

KRITA

A free and open source digital painting application focused on providing a comprehensive toolset for illustrators and concept artists.

For the Author-Strategist: For an author who is also an illustrator, Krita is a top tier tool for creating original cover art or interior illustrations. Otherwise, it is a tool to be aware of when hiring freelance illustrators.

For the Author-Technologist: For authors with artistic skills, Krita is often preferred over GIMP for creating illustrated covers due to its focus on the digital painting process. Its advanced brush engines and color management integrate well into a FOSS design workflow with Inkscape and Scribus.

Key Features: World class digital brush engines, non-destructive editing through filter layers and masks, advanced color management, animation tools, cross platform.

Platform Availability: Windows, macOS, Linux, Android.

BOOK BRUSH

A web based design platform specifically created for authors to easily produce professional marketing graphics, including 3D book mockups and social media ads.

For the Author-Strategist: A high leverage tool that directly addresses marketing needs. The ability to quickly create dozens of high-quality promotional images (e.g., a book cover on a phone, tablet, or in a scene) provides an excellent return on time invested.

For the Author-Technologist: While a technologist could create 3D mockups in a tool like Blender, the speed and template-driven nature of Book

Brush make it a pragmatic and efficient choice for marketing tasks. It auto-mates a complex design job, freeing up time.

Key Features: Massive library of author-centric templates, one-click 3D book mockup generator, video effects for ads, direct integration with social media platforms.

Platform Availability: Web.

21

PUBLISHING TOOLS

These tools include traditional desktop publishing style products, but also tools that can be overlooked such as ways to produce audiobooks (Eleven-Labs/Audacity), or deliver your book as a packaged application (PWA). Self-publishers have the ability to do so much more today.

VELLUM

A specialized macOS application designed exclusively for creating beautifully formatted, professional-grade ebook and print book interiors with minimal effort.

For the Author-Strategist: The premier tool for maximizing speed-to-market for fiction and simple non-fiction. The cost is easily justified by the immense time savings compared to manual formatting. It produces consistently excellent results, allowing the author to focus on writing and marketing.

For the Author-Technologist: A "black box" that abstracts away granular control, but its efficiency is undeniable. It's a pragmatic tool for optimizing a workflow, automating tedious tasks like widow/orphan control and guaranteeing valid, platform-compliant ebook files every time.

Key Features: One click generation for all major ebook/print formats, library of professional built in book styles, live preview across multiple device types, automatic error correction.

Platform Availability: macOS.

ATTICUS

A web-based and desktop application for writing, formatting, and creating professional grade ebook and print book interiors, positioned as a cross-platform alternative to Vellum.

For the Author-Strategist: The best Vellum alternative for Windows and Linux users, and a strong competitor overall. The feature gap has narrowed significantly, with Atticus offering a robust, built in theme builder for custom styles. The choice is now less about features and more about ecosystem preference: a native macOS app (Vellum) vs. a cross-platform web and desktop app (Atticus).

For the Author-Technologist: An interesting all-in-one tool that attempts to span the entire writing and production workflow. While its GUI based approach doesn't lend itself to a "Book as Code" pipeline, its cross-platform nature and robust feature set make it a noteworthy tool for those who need Vellum-like results outside the Apple ecosystem.

Key Features: Cross-platform (Windows, macOS, Linux, Web), combines writing and formatting, built in theme builder for custom styles, real time preview, goal setting and writing habit tracker.

Platform Availability: Windows, macOS, Linux, Web.

SCRIBUS

A powerful, open source desktop publishing application that provides a free alternative to Adobe InDesign and Affinity Publisher for complex page layout.

For the Author-Strategist: A viable option for visually complex books (e.g., children's books, cookbooks) when the budget is zero and the author is willing to invest significant time in learning. Strategically, it's a tool to consider only when cost saving is the absolute highest priority.

For the Author-Technologist: The primary open-source tool for graphical page layout. It provides the necessary professional features, including CMYK color management, vector drawing tools, and press-ready PDF/X export. It is the cornerstone of a FOSS publishing workflow for visually complex projects.

Key Features: No cost, professional DTP features (CMYK, master pages, bleed management), cross-platform availability, robust PDF export options.

Platform Availability: Windows, macOS, Linux.

PANDOC

A universal, command line document converter that can read numerous input formats (especially Markdown) and write to dozens of output formats, including EPUB, DOCX, and PDF.

For the Author-Strategist: Not a tool for direct use. It is the invisible "engine" inside other systems. Understanding that Pandoc exists is strategically useful to know that automated, high quality format conversion is a solved problem.

For the Author-Technologist: The single most important tool in the entire "Book as Code" ecosystem. It is the central hub that transforms a collection of simple Markdown files into any professional format required. It is scriptable, extensible, and provides absolute control over the entire conversion and typesetting process.

Key Features: Converts between dozens of file formats, extensive Markdown support (including citations, tables, footnotes), powerful templating system, filter support for custom extensions (e.g., using Lua).

Platform Availability: Windows, macOS, Linux (command-line).

LaTeX

A high quality typesetting system and document preparation language, often used as a backend by Pandoc to create professional, publication-quality PDFs.

For the Author-Strategist: Not for direct use. It is the "engine" that creates the beautiful typography in academic papers and professionally typeset books. A strategist only needs to appreciate the high-quality output it produces.

For the Author-Technologist: The ultimate tool for typographic control in an automated workflow. By creating a custom LaTeX template, a technologist can define every aspect of a book's design in code. Margins, fonts, headers, chapter headings, you name it. This ensures perfect consistency and producing PDFs that are superior to those from standard word processors.

Key Features: Unparalleled typographic quality, programmable macros for automation, robust handling of complex documents (cross references, bibliographies), separation of content and presentation.

Platform Availability: Windows (MiKTeX), macOS (MacTeX), Linux (TeX Live).

ELEVENLABS

An AI voice synthesis and cloning platform that produces incredibly realistic, emotionally nuanced text-to-speech audio.

For the Author-Strategist: This is a revolutionary tool that drastically lowers the barrier to entry for audiobook production. As of 2025, the platform includes a "Projects" feature, allowing you to manage an entire book's worth of audio files, and offers even more granular control over voice emotion and pacing. You can create a professional sounding audiobook for a fraction of the cost of a human narrator, opening up a vital revenue stream.

For the Author-Technologist: An API driven audio generation engine. The work is in preparing clean, well-structured text (SSML is your friend here) and scripting the process to render an entire novel chapter by chapter. You can build a fully automated pipeline: Pandoc converts Markdown to clean text, which is then fed to the ElevenLabs API, and the resulting audio files are compiled and tagged.

Key Features: Hyper realistic AI voices, voice cloning from short samples, precise control over pacing and emotion, API for programmatic generation.

Platform Availability: Web.

Prompt Example:

> **Technologist:** "Write a Python script that takes a plain text file as input, splits it into chunks of 2,000 characters, and sends each chunk to the ElevenLabs API using my API key. The script should use a specific voice ID, save each resulting MP3 file sequentially, and include error handling for API timeouts."

Audacity

A free, open source, cross-platform digital audio editor. It is the long standing FOSS standard for audio recording and editing.

For the Author-Strategist: The no cost entry point for narrating your own audiobooks or starting a podcast. If you choose not to use AI, this is the tool you'll most likely use to record, edit, and master your audio files to meet the technical specifications of platforms like Audible.

For the Author-Technologist: The GIMP/Scribus of the audio world. It's a powerful, scriptable (via Nyquist) audio workstation that fits perfectly into a FOSS production pipeline. It's used for cleaning up audio, applying compression and EQ, and batch processing files for final delivery.

Key Features: Multi-track audio recording and editing, noise reduction filters, extensive effects library, audio analysis tools, scriptable.

Platform Availability: Windows, macOS, Linux.

PWA (Progressive Web App)

An application delivered through the web, built using web technologies, intended to provide an app like experience including offline capabilities and home screen installation.

For the Author-Strategist: An interesting, though niche, delivery mechanism. A PWA could be used to create a unique, immersive reading experience for a specific book, complete with interactive elements not possible in a standard ebook. A high effort strategy for a specific artistic or marketing goal.

For the Author-Technologist: A software architecture. This is a project to be built. A technologist author with web dev skills might build a PWA to serialize their novel directly to readers, bypassing retailers and maintaining full control over the user experience.

Key Features: Works offline, installable on a user's home screen, accessible via a URL, can deliver push notifications.

Platform Availability: Any modern web browser (cross-platform).

22

AUTHOR PLATFORM AND MARKETING

Tools specific to building websites are located in the "Website and Socials" section even though they could also be considered part of the author platform and marketing tools.

GUMROAD / LEMON SQUEEZY

E-commerce platforms built for creators to sell digital products directly to their audience.

For the Author-Strategist: This is how you build a resilient, high-margin author business. As of 2025, Lemon Squeezy has become a preferred option for many authors due to its robust, automated handling of global sales tax (like VAT) and its built-in affiliate program features. Gumroad remains an excellent, simple-to-use alternative. The strategy is to sell your books directly, offer exclusive bundles, and keep a much larger percentage of the revenue.

For the Author-Technologist: These are API first platforms that handle all the complexities of global e-commerce: payment processing, sales tax, VAT, and secure file delivery. Your job is to integrate their "buy" buttons or APIs into your static author website. This creates a powerful, low cost sales channel that you control completely.

Key Features: Simple digital product setup, handles global sales tax/VAT, secure file hosting and delivery, customizable landing pages, analytics.

Platform Availability: Web.

Squarespace

An all-in-one, premium website builder known for its award-winning design templates and ease of use.

For the Author-Strategist: The "it just works" solution for a beautiful, professional author website without needing to touch code. It combines hosting, domains, e-commerce, and email marketing in one package. This is the strategic choice for authors who value a polished brand image and want to minimize time spent on technical management.

For the Author-Technologist: A "walled garden." While aesthetically pleasing, it offers limited access to the underlying code, making deep customization or integration with external build processes difficult. A technologist would likely feel constrained by its GUI-driven nature and lack of shell access.

Key Features: Professionally designed templates, drag and drop editor, integrated e-commerce and marketing tools, reliable hosting included.

Platform Availability: Web.

WIX

A popular website builder that offers a high degree of design freedom through a free form, unstructured editor and a large app marketplace.

For the Author-Strategist: A flexible and accessible option, particularly with its free tier entry point. Its AI-powered "ADI" (Artificial Design Intelligence) can generate a starter site quickly. Good for authors who want a highly visual, customized site and enjoy a more hands-on, drag and drop design process.

For the Author-Technologist: Similar to Squarespace, it's a closed ecosystem that abstracts away the code. The unstructured editor can create less than optimal code on the backend, which can be frustrating. The value is in its API and app market, which may allow for some limited integration.

Key Features: Free-form drag-and-drop editor, Wix ADI for AI assisted site creation, large App Market for extending functionality, free plan available.

Platform Availability: Web.

Prompt Example:

> **Strategist (for the Wix ADI):** "Create a website for a thriller author named Jane Colt. The style should be modern, sharp, and suspenseful, using a black, white, and crimson red color palette. I need a homepage featuring my latest novel, an 'About' page, a page for my book series, and a contact form."

HUGO

An extremely fast, modern static site generator built in Go, distributed as a single binary for simple installation and use.

For the Author-Strategist: The platform for an author who values website performance and security. A Hugo site is incredibly fast, which improves SEO and user experience. It's a "build it once, run it forever" asset that can be hosted for free and handle massive launch-day traffic spikes without issue.

For the Author-Technologist: The superior choice for performance and dependency management. The single binary (no Node.js, Ruby, etc.) is trivial to use in any CI/CD pipeline. Its "batteries-included" features like on-the-fly image processing provide immense power without managing fragile plugins.

Key Features: Millisecond build speeds, single executable file for installation, powerful built-in image processing, robust module system, free hosting on platforms like Netlify.

Platform Availability: Windows, macOS, Linux (command-line).

JEKYLL

The original, blog-aware static site generator built with Ruby, known for its maturity and seamless integration with GitHub Pages.

For the Author-Strategist: The most direct path to a functional, free, and reliable author website. The key advantage is its zero configuration integration with GitHub Pages, write a post, push the file, and the site is live. The vast library of themes allows for a professional look with minimal effort.

For the Author-Technologist: An ecosystem-driven choice. While slower than Hugo, its flexibility comes from a massive library of Ruby plugins (Gems). Managing the environment with Bundler is a core task, but it provides a highly customizable platform, especially for those comfortable in the Ruby ecosystem.

Key Features: Native, seamless integration with GitHub Pages, vast and mature ecosystem of plugins and themes, powerful Liquid templating language, strong community support.

Platform Availability: Windows, macOS, Linux (requires a Ruby development environment).

Hugging Face Spaces

A versatile cloud platform for building, deploying, and hosting AI-powered applications in containerized environments, supporting custom Docker containers and persistent storage.

For the Author-Strategist: A platform for building an author's *entire* digital presence. By 2025, Spaces offers a library of one-click apps that make it accessible to non-coders. You can deploy a fine-tuned character chatbot or a lore Q&A bot with minimal technical skill, creating a powerful engagement tool for your website.

For the Author-Technologist: The introduction of custom Docker support is the single most important feature. You can deploy any web app (Go, Rust, Node.js) in a container. Persistent storage allows for stateful applications like a website with a user database, making it a Heroku like PaaS for AI workloads.

Key Features: Custom Docker container support, Git-based deployment, scalable hardware (CPU/GPU), persistent storage options, built-in secrets management.

Platform Availability: Development on Windows, macOS, or Linux. Deployed applications are web-based.

DeepSite

An AI-powered website generator that creates functional websites from a single text prompt.

For the Author-Strategist: A powerful "speed-to-market" tool for creating a Version 1.0 website. This approach allows for rapid prototyping and validation of marketing ideas without upfront development cost. New tools in this space are releasing at a fast clip, be sure to check for other options.

For the Author-Technologist: A powerful AI assisted scaffolding tool. It generates the "first draft" of the codebase. A technologist uses it to save hours of initial HTML/CSS coding, then downloads the source to begin the real work of customization, integration, and deployment in a proper Git workflow.

Key Features: Single-prompt website generation, full source code export (HTML, CSS, JS), rapid prototyping, powered by state-of-the-art LLMs.

Platform Availability: The generator is a web based tool; the output is a platform-agnostic website codebase.

Prompt Example:

> **Strategist (as the prompt for DeepSite):** "Create a one page author website for me, [Author Name]. I write epic fantasy. The design should be immersive and use a parchment paper background texture with a dark fantasy font. It needs four sections: a hero image with my latest book cover and a tagline, a short bio section with my photo, a gallery of

my other books with links to buy, and a simple email signup form."

MAILCHIMP

A well established, all-in-one email marketing platform that includes CRM, landing pages, and automation features.

For the Author-Strategist: The easy to start, widely known option for building a mailing list. Its user friendly interface is great for beginners. It's a good choice for authors who want a single platform for email, landing pages, and simple automations, but be aware that costs escalate significantly as your list grows.

For the Author-Technologist: An API driven service. A technologist will interact with it programmatically to automate signups from a custom built website. The audience based list management can feel restrictive compared to more modern, tag-based systems.

Key Features: Email marketing and automation, simple landing page builder, basic CRM functionality, widely used and recognized.

Platform Availability: Web.

CONVERTKIT

An email marketing platform built specifically for professional creators like authors, focusing on powerful automations and a tag-based subscriber system.

For the Author-Strategist: The recommended choice for authors serious about building a business. Its powerful visual automations and flexible tagging allow you to segment readers effectively and send them highly relevant content, which is key to building a loyal fanbase and driving sales.

For the Author-Technologist: A superior platform from an architectural standpoint. The tag based system is more logical and easier to manage programmatically via its flexible API than Mailchimp's audiences. It is better suited for building complex, automated marketing funnels.

Key Features: Creator focused platform, powerful visual automations, flexible tag/segment based system, integrated digital product sales and paid newsletters.

Platform Availability: Web.

LISTMONK

A high performance, open source, self-hosted email marketing and newsletter platform.

For the Author-Strategist: Not recommended for direct use. This is a strategic decision approved by the strategist but implemented by the technologist. The goal is to dramatically reduce costs at scale (tens of thousands of subscribers), with the trade off being the upfront time and cost of setup and ongoing maintenance.

For the Author-Technologist: The ultimate FOSS solution for mailing lists. It's a single Go binary that's incredibly performant. You host it yourself (e.g., on a cheap VPS or a Raspberry Pi) and use a separate SMTP relay service like Amazon SES to send emails for a fraction of the cost of SaaS tools. You get total control and data ownership, but you are responsible for everything.

Key Features: Self hosted and open source, no subscriber/email limits, high performance (Go), API-first design, works with any SMTP provider.

Platform Availability: Linux server (command-line/Docker).

Prompt Example:

> **Technologist:** "I'm setting up Listmonk with Amazon SES for sending emails. Provide the AWS IAM policy JSON required to create a user with the minimum necessary permissions (`ses:SendRawEmail`) to act as the SMTP credential provider for Listmonk."

NETGALLEY / BOOKSIRENS / BOOKSPROUT

Services that connect authors with a community of reviewers to facilitate the distribution of ARCs (Advance Reader Copies).

For the Author-Strategist: Essential marketing channels for generating early buzz and securing reviews before a book's launch. The strategy involves choosing the platform(s) that best match the book's genre and the author's budget to maximize pre-launch reviews.

For the Author-Technologist: Distribution endpoints. The task is to ensure that the ebook files (EPUB, MOBI) are correctly formatted, validated, and securely uploaded to these platforms according to their specific technical requirements.

Key Features: ARC distribution to a large reviewer pool, reviewer feedback management, tools to prevent piracy, optional marketing features.

Platform Availability: Web.

BookBub

A powerful book discovery platform that sends daily emails to millions of readers about discounted ebooks.

For the Author-Strategist: Landing a BookBub Featured Deal is one of the most effective marketing tactics in self-publishing. The platform is also critical for advertising (BookBub Ads) and generating pre-launch buzz (New Release Alerts).

For the Author-Technologist: A marketing platform with specific technical requirements for ad images, book metadata, and linking. The job is to ensure all assets provided to the platform are optimized for performance and meet BookBub's exacting standards.

Key Features: Highly curated Featured Deals, pay-per-click ad platform, author profile pages, new release alerts for followers, book recommendations.

Platform Availability: Web.

Publisher Rocket

A desktop software application that helps authors research Amazon keywords, categories, and competitors.

For the Author-Strategist: A critical market research tool. It provides the data needed to make informed decisions about which keywords and categories to target, directly impacting a book's visibility and sales potential on Amazon.

For the Author-Technologist: A data scraping and analysis application. It automates the process of gathering and interpreting Amazon sales data, presenting it in a structured way for analysis.

Key Features: Keyword search analysis, category research tool, competitor analysis, Amazon ad keyword generator.

Platform Availability: Windows, macOS.

Royal Road

An online platform for web fiction and serialized novels, popular in genres like LitRPG and Progression Fantasy.

For the Author-Strategist: A key platform for building an audience *before* a traditional ebook launch. By posting chapters serially, authors can gather a large following and get immediate reader feedback, building a powerful launch-day audience.

For the Author-Technologist: A content management system (CMS) for serialized fiction. Some authors develop scripts to automate the formatting and posting process from their primary manuscript source (e.g., from Markdown files).

Key Features: Serialized story hosting, reader feedback and commenting, author donation integration (e.g., Patreon), genre-specific discovery algorithms.

Platform Availability: Web.

BookFunnel / StoryOrigin

Services designed for secure ebook delivery, reader magnet hosting, newsletter swaps with other authors, and managing review copy distribution.

For the Author-Strategist: Core marketing infrastructure. These platforms are the most effective way to grow a newsletter mailing list (via reader magnets) and to cross promote with other authors in the same genre.

For the Author-Technologist: Secure, reliable delivery APIs. These services solve the complex technical problem of delivering digital files to a wide variety of devices and email clients, providing a robust, pre-built solution.

Key Features: Secure ebook/audiobook delivery, landing pages for reader magnets, newsletter swap and group promotion marketplaces.

Platform Availability: Web.

BOOKSTAGRAM / BOOKTOK

These are communities on Instagram and TikTok, respectively, that are dedicated to books, reading, and reviewing.

For the Author-Strategist: Vital marketing *channels*. A strategist develops a content plan to engage with readers and influencers on these platforms, using visual assets and short-form video to build a brand.

For the Author-Technologist: Content delivery networks for visual media. The role is to produce or acquire the high quality visual assets needed, ensuring they are correctly formatted, compressed, and optimized for mobile viewing.

Key Features: (As platforms) Short-form video (TikTok), image and video sharing (Instagram), large communities of active readers, influencer marketing.

Platform Availability: iOS, Android, Web.

In design area, but also very important here:

GOOGLE MAKERSUITE / VERTEX AI

Google AI Studio App Builder is listed in the design section, but it's worth mentioning here too as it is useful as a **component generator**. It is not designed to build a full website, but can create interactive AI-powered *modules* or *widgets* that you embed within or link from your main author website (which would be built on any of the other platforms mentioned in this section). An author magnet component could be developed here and added to your website as one example.

See the description in the **design** section for more details.

23

Brainstorming and Collaboration

Miro / Mural

Virtual, infinite digital whiteboard platforms designed for real time visual collaboration.

For the Strategist: Miro is a highly recommended tool for you. It's perfect for visually mapping out plot timelines, character relationships, or the flow of a non-fiction book without the constraints of a linear word processor. It is the ideal platform for conducting a remote Cover Design Workshop with a hired designer, allowing you both to build a mood board and brainstorm concepts collaboratively. The intuitive, drag and drop interface requires no technical expertise.

For the Technologist: While you can create text-based mind maps and diagrams with code, Miro offers a different, often more fluid and creative, mode of thinking. It is the recommended tool for high-level system architecture and workflow planning (e.g., mapping out your entire Pandoc build process visually before you write the scripts). It is also an invaluable tool for collaborating with non-technical stakeholders (like the Strategist or an external editor).

Key Features: Infinite digital white-boarding, extensive template libraries, real-time collaboration, and a powerful suite of AI features for automatically generating diagrams, clustering sticky notes, and expanding on ideas.

Platform Availability: Web, Windows, macOS, iOS, Android.

xMɪɴᴅ

A dedicated, full-featured mind-mapping and brainstorming application.

For the Author-Strategist: An excellent tool for solo brainstorming and structuring ideas. It's perfect for breaking down a complex novel into its core components or outlining a non-fiction book's structure. More structured and focused than a free form whiteboard.

For the Author-Technologist: A structured data visualization tool. Useful for creating hierarchical outlines of codebases, planning documentation structure, or breaking down a complex problem. Its ability to export to formats like Markdown is a key feature for workflow integration.

Key Features: Professional mind mapping, organizational charts, timelines, multiple themes and styles, export to various formats (PDF, PNG, Markdown).

Platform Availability: Windows, macOS, Linux, iOS, Android.

Prompt Example:

> **Strategist:** "I need to outline a new book series. Create a mind map structure for me in a format that I can build in xMind. The central topic is 'The Sunstone Chronicles'. The main branches should be: `Series Arc`, `Book 1 Plot`, `Main Characters`, `Worldbuilding`, and `Magic System`. Populate each branch with at least three relevant sub-topics."

TRELLO

A Kanban style project management tool that uses boards, lists, and cards to organize tasks and workflows visually.

For the Author-Strategist: The ideal tool for managing the entire publishing process as a visual project. It can be used to track tasks from drafting (To Do list) to editing (In Progress list) to publication (Done list), ensuring no critical steps are missed.

For the Author-Technologist: A visual front end for a project's task list. Its API allows for integration into automated workflows. For example, a git push to the main branch could trigger a script that automatically moves a "Finalize Chapter" card to the "Done" list.

Key Features: Visual Kanban boards, task cards with checklists and due dates, collaboration features, automation ("Butler"), integration with other services.

Platform Availability: Web, Windows, macOS, iOS, Android.

ASANA

A comprehensive work management platform designed for team collaboration, allowing for the creation of tasks, projects, and calendars with a focus on timelines and dependencies.

For the Author-Strategist: A more robust alternative to Trello, suitable for authors managing a large backlist, a team (editor, designer, PA), or a complex marketing strategy. Its Timeline and Calendar views are excellent for planning long-term launch schedules.

For the Author-Technologist: A highly structured project management system. Its power lies in managing dependencies (e.g., "cover design cannot start until final blurb is written"). Its extensive API allows for more sophisticated automation than Trello.

Key Features: Multiple project views (list, board, timeline, calendar), task dependencies, goal tracking, team management, detailed reporting.

Platform Availability: Web, iOS, Android.

PINTEREST

A visual discovery engine where users find ideas and inspiration through images and videos known as "Pins," often used for creating inspiration boards.

For the Author-Strategist: An excellent tool for visual brainstorming (e.g., creating a private "mood board" for a new book's characters, locations, and aesthetics) and for marketing to specific demographics with compelling, shareable visual Pins.

For the Author-Technologist: A content delivery network with a focus on image metadata and SEO. The task is to optimize images with specific keywords, descriptions, and rich data to maximize their discoverability within Pinterest's search algorithm.

Key Features: Visual "pinboards," image and video sharing, powerful search and discovery algorithm, long lifespan for content.

Platform Availability: Web, iOS, Android.

24

RELATED AUTHORING DISCIPLINES AND TOOLS

This section lists tools and topics that are adjacent to the core book publishing workflow, serving as a resource for future projects or skill expansion.

PRESENTATION TOOLS

Marp / Beamer

"Slides as Code" software for creating presentations. Beamer is a LaTeX class for academic quality PDFs, while Marp is a simple, modern tool that uses Markdown to create presentations in HTML or PDF.

For the Author-Strategist: Niche tools for creating materials for book talks, workshops, or online courses related to the author's books or expertise. The output is a professional slide deck for public speaking.

For the Author-Technologist: The proper way to create and version presentations. Beamer is for LaTeX/PDF workflows, integrating with a Pandoc toolchain. Marp is excellent for web native presentations due to its simplicity and first class VS Code extension, allowing for version control in Git and easy hosting.

Key Features: (Beamer) High quality typography, LaTeX integration. (Marp) Web-native, simple Markdown syntax, excellent VS Code integration.

Platform Availability: (Beamer) Any LaTeX distribution. (Marp) As a VS-Codium/VSCode extension or command line tool.

CATEGORY: WORKFLOW AUTOMATION & INTEGRATION

These are the "digital duct tape" tools that connect your other systems, creating a seamless, automated workflow.

n8n (pronounced "nodemation")

An open-source, self hostable workflow automation tool that provides a visual, node based interface for connecting different applications and APIs. The FOSS alternative to Zapier.

For the Author-Strategist: Not for direct use, but for defining the desired outcome. The strategist says: "I want a system where, after I publish a new blog post on my Hugo site, it automatically posts a link to Twitter and creates a draft campaign in ConvertKit." This tool is the engine that makes that happen.

For the Author-Technologist: The central nervous system of your automated publishing empire. You run n8n in a Docker container and use it to connect everything: a new `git push` to your book's repository can trigger a Pandoc build, upload the new file to a Dropbox folder, and send you a notification on Discord. It's the ultimate "glue" for your entire toolchain.

Key Features: Visual workflow editor, self-hostable for control and cost savings, hundreds of pre-built nodes for popular services, can run custom code (JS/Python).

Platform Availability: Self-hosted via Docker (Linux server) or a paid cloud version.

Prompt Example:

> **Technologist:** "Design a workflow in n8n. The trigger is a new RSS feed item from my blog. The first step is to shorten the item's URL using a Bitly node. The second step is to use the shortened URL in a post to the Twitter API. The final step is to send the original blog post title and URL to a Discord webhook."

ADDITIONAL TECHNOLOGIST INFRASTRUCTURE

For the Author-Technologist who wants a truly professional, reproducible, and scalable "Book as Code" system.

Docker/Devbox Containers

Containerization technology that allows you to package an application and its entire environment into a single, isolated unit. Everything like libraries, dependencies, specific versions of software, and configuration files.

For the Author-Strategist: The benefit is indirect but massive: reliability and speed. Your technologist partner uses Docker to ensure that the "book factory" they've built will work flawlessly, every time, on any computer, forever. It eliminates the risk of "it broke after an update."

For the Author-Technologist: This is the core of a professional, reproducible build environment. You could choose to install Pandoc, LaTeX, and Python into a Docker container instead of on your host OS. For example, with Docker you define your entire toolchain in a `Dockerfile`. Anyone (including your future self) can then `git pull` your repository, build the container,

159

and be guaranteed to have the exact same environment, eliminating all "it works on my machine" problems. I use a container to run Qdrant database supporting RAG for my book projects as another example.

Key Features: OS-level virtualization, reproducible environments, dependency isolation, portable and lightweight.

Platform Availability: Windows, macOS, Linux.

Git LFS (Large File Storage)

An open-source extension for Git that replaces large files (like audio, video, and high-resolution design files) with text pointers inside Git, while storing the file contents on a remote server. If you have video and audio files associated with your books, this could become an important part of your workflow.

For the Author-Strategist: An organizational tool that allows *all* project assets like the manuscript, the massive cover art PSD file, the audiobook WAV files, to live together in one version controlled project, without breaking the system.

For the Author-Technologist: A critical tool that solves one of Git's fundamental weaknesses: handling large binary files. This allows you to properly version your Affinity Publisher files, audiobook masters, and other multi megabyte assets right alongside your Markdown manuscript, creating a truly unified and versioned source of truth for the entire project.

Key Features: Integrates with Git workflow, handles large binary files efficiently, supports various remote storage backends.

Platform Availability: Windows, macOS, Linux (Git extension).

Google NotebookLM

An AI powered research and writing assistant that is grounded in the user's own source documents.

For the Author-Strategist: This is your personal, expert research assistant. You can upload your entire manuscript, character notes, and research articles. You can then ask it complex questions ("What was the name of the tavern in Chapter 3 and did I ever describe its owner?"), have it generate summaries of your plot, or ask it to create a timeline of events. It only answers based on the sources you provide, making it a powerful tool for maintaining consistency and quickly finding information.

For the Author-Technologist: A private, self contained Retrieval Augmented Generation (RAG) system. It provides a simple interface for grounding a powerful LLM on a specific corpus of documents without needing to build a complex software pipeline. This is ideal for creating a private "lore keeper" or a technical documentation expert without any coding.

Key Features: Grounded AI responses based on user-provided sources, ability to synthesize information across multiple documents, generates summaries, outlines, and timelines, private and secure.

Platform Availability: Web.

25

Choose Your Tools! Viewpoints

There is a clear divergence in optimal workflows based on the author's primary persona and the nature of their project. We've been talking about self publishing from two primary perspectives.

For the **Strategist**, typically the primary driver is time to market and return on investment. The ideal toolchain is often a hybrid approach. For example, **Canva** for rapid creation of marketing materials and **Vellum** for efficient and beautiful interior formatting. For more complex projects, the strategist will likely outsource the design to a professional designer, rather than investing the time to learn those tools themselves.

For the **Technologist**, the core driver is control, customization, and often, a preference for open source and scriptable tools. Their ideal workflow might involve writing the manuscript in a plain text format like Markdown, using a "Diagrams as Code" approach for any illustrations, and then using a combination of **Scribus, GIMP, and Inkscape** for the final layout and cover design. This approach allows for a completely version controlled, automated, and low-cost publishing pipeline.

The most significant trend in this space is the rise of specialized, user friendly tools that abstract away the complexities of traditional design software. **Vellum and Book Brush** are prime examples of this, targeting the specific needs of authors and offering a significant speed advantage.

Ultimately, the most effective system is one that is tailored to your own skills and the project's requirements. A fiction author with a straightforward manuscript will have a very different "optimal" toolchain than a technical author writing a book with numerous diagrams and code samples. The key is to consciously choose the right tools for the job, rather than defaulting to the most well known or most powerful option.

It can be useful to think a bit differently about how you design your workflow and how to decide which tools to use for projects. Below I've laid out some viewpoints that might inspire you to try something different than what you may have done in the past.

There are many examples is this section that are technical in nature, or utilizing different tools than might be the traditional choices, but do not discount the power of simple things as well.

I offer this prime example: During the process of researching this book, I started as I had with previous projects with one large document. And also like on so many previous projects I quickly started having trouble keeping track of everything. I did eventually fall into a new mindset which led me to adopt many new ways of working. The most profound example is actually one that is so simple I don't know why I hadn't already started using it years ago. I broke up my book into many smaller files. In the past I had used Libreoffice Writer or other some other word processor. I found it very difficult to manage once I got past a few chapters.

I started researching how others put together their projects. I found that there is a whole standard around frontmatter, mainmatter, and backmatter that was already in place for the book industry. This structure just so happens to work perfectly with many small files. This structure also works well for automation, so I put together a template I could use over and over again.

In case you hadn't already noticed, I fall further towards the **technologist** side of that equation, so I wrote some code to build out a structure for me. I will cover my own personal system as an example later in this book, but for now let's get on with some specific ideas of how you might adopt a different viewpoint to possibly find some new ways of working or adopt some new tools that could make you more productive.

I encourage you to try anything here that makes you curious, but not to spend too much time on things that don't click with you right away. You can always fall back to what you know will keep you moving forward on your writing projects.

VIEWPOINT: THE HISTORY HOLDER (ORGANIZATION):

An author can create an app, grounded on their notes and world documents, and use it as a personal "Lore Keeper" to quickly check for consistency. For example: "What was the name of the tavern mentioned in Chapter 3 of Book 1?" This is faster than manually searching through documents and helps prevent continuity errors.

That app could be built in several ways that would allow you to take advantage of AI tooling to get answers from your own documents. One such method would take a form of a "notebook". Google offers a tool called NotebookLM (covered in the tools list) that is free to use for individuals with a Google account. The free version lets you upload up to 50 of your own documents and then you can ask questions utilizing the AI. This product will also generate a podcast style output to talk to you about the contents, generate mind maps, and more. I've found it immensely helpful in so many use cases, not just related to book development.

VIEWPOINT: THE FORMATTING EDITOR (EDITING)

If you decided to use Pandoc and LaTeX for formatting your book, you could upload the documentation for those tools into NotebookLM and ask questions about how to do formatting you need. You can even add in your current configurations so you can get code specific directions back to work out issues. Is it perfect? No, but I used this very system when developing my custom tex template I created for formatting this book.

You can throw all the pdf manuals for the software you use in a NotebookLM notebook and then ask questions about how to do things.

For example, I added manuals for Pandoc and KOMA Script, and srcbook to great effect. KOMA Script and srcbook are specialized LaTeX packages I use, if you love everything about intricate details of formatting your books, you'll want to research the LaTeX ecosystem. The formatting in this book comes from a custom LaTeX format that I couldn't have developed without this tool to help me dive into the complexities of formatting, the manuals alone are hundreds of pages long, finding that one specific detail is so much faster when you have these in a notebook. Plus the other cool thing is the ability to relate two disparate tools together by having both their manuals in the same notebook. NotebookLM will catch the crossover very well in my experience. I wrote this book in markdown (a text format) and used Pandoc to covert to LaTeX based on a template I created with help from "asking questions" to NotebookLM with the manuals all as sources in a notebook.

VIEWPOINT: THE MARKETING CONTENT ENGINE (PLATFORM AND MARKETING):

An author can create an app grounded on their book's themes, characters, and plot, then prompt it to "Generate five tweets about the moral dilemma my protagonist faces." This creates an on-brand, tireless brainstorming partner for generating social media content.

Key Features: No-code prompt-based interface, data grounding (RAG) via file uploads, generates embeddable/shareable web app links, powered by Google's Gemini models or some other top model of your choice. There are free tiers on most of the bigger players in this space, check the terms of service before using for content you expect to copyright (probably not a problem for tweets, but you get the idea).

Platform Availability: Web.

Viewpoint: The Interactive Author Website

HuggingFace Spaces

A platform for coding, deploying, and hosting complete, custom-built AI-powered web applications, including full author websites with unique, integrated AI features.

For the Author-Strategist:

This is the platform for creating an ultimate, destination author website that is an experience in itself. Imagine a site where fans can not only read about your world but also generate unique character portraits based on your descriptions (using a fine-tuned image model) or co-write a short piece of fan fiction with an AI trained in your style. This is a significant investment to build a powerful, long term brand asset.

For the Author-Technologist:

This provides the full stack for an AI native author site. A technologist can build a Python backend using a framework like FastAPI, fine tune an open source LLM (like Llama 3) on their entire backlist, create a front-end with Streamlit or Gradio, and host the entire application on a Space. This allows for total control, enabling features impossible with no-code solutions, such as chaining multiple models together or connecting to external databases. The challenge I have with an option like this one is the control factor, you have to decide whether you like being dependent on a platform that is in a rapidly evolving state and that could change features to potentially remove something you have come to depend on. I think this is true of almost any platform, but ones in the AI space are changing even more rapidly than anywhere else. As some perspective, in the time between when I started writing this book to when I was finished (about three months), I had to re-write several sections right at the end to account for all the change that had already taken place. I discuss more details of this in several places through the book, you can work with it if you prepare for it with local backups and are quick to research new or upcoming options. It's a process to stay relevant as a self published author.

VIEWPOINT: THE BESPOKE WRITING ASSISTANT (WRITING AND EDITING):

For the Author-Technologist:

A technologist can fine tune a powerful language model on their own prose to create a true writing assistant that understands their specific narrative voice, character mannerisms, and stylistic tics. This goes beyond simple Q&A; it's a tool that can help draft paragraphs or suggest dialogue that is verifiably *in-character* and *in-style*. There are some serious challenges with this and I did not do this myself, doing fine tuning would typically require you to rent expensive GPUS to do the training, and a PC with expensive GPU boards to be able to run the model locally, or pay to host GPUs to run it for you. Check into builder communities on ollama.com or others to start communicating with others if you want to learn about how to do this.

For Both Personas:

I recommend a slightly different approach. I feel it's more prudent to work with one of the big commercial models and have an iterative discussion about your chosen voice. This will save you a lot of time just getting the technology to do what you need it to do.

In a prompt, describe what you like and don't like, the emotion you want to evoke in different situations, and so forth. Recently I did this for a fantasy novel I was dusting off and I wanted apply a more consistent voice to my writing, to keep me more "in character". Think of it as defining a distinct literary persona. The author Fernado Pessoa made this popular, and I've adopted the process for my novels, he would develop distinct voices he called heteronyms for characters in his books. I started with a prompt to an LLM telling about the qualities I wanted in my persona, and added more and more through iterations until I was satisfied, now I can refer to the heteronym I created whenever working on that book to get back into character.

Prompt Example:

> "Acting as an expert author and writer, create a heteronym in the concept made popular by Fernado Pessoa. Focus on these qualities below, I want to roll these qualities into logical heteronyms. Roll these up to 3, or tell why I need more. [list qualities of your favorite authors, or your own styling, example From Martin Amis: Linguistic inventiveness, satirical explorations.]"

Viewpoint: The Multimedia Factory:

For the Author-Strategist:

If your primary goal is to efficiently produce high quality audiobooks with a user friendly interface and without the need for deep technical intervention, Eleven Labs is the clear winner. Its dedicated audiobook creation tools and vast library of voices make it a powerful asset for creation of audio books. You can even use different voices for the characters in your books if you wish. I found this tool to be very easy to use and a worthy option, but there is a cost. I found that the limited free plan was only enough credits to convert one chapter to audio, but their subscription options are fairly affordable.

For the Author-Technologist:

HuggingFace Spaces that was mentioned earlier can host more than just text based models. An author could deploy an open source text-to-speech model (like Tortoise TTS) and train it on their own voice to generate free, high-quality audio samples for marketing. Or they could fine tune a Stable Diffusion model on concept art to create an endless stream of on brand visuals for social media. There are other options like Chatterbox that have online direct use options, still technical but not as in depth as setting up Tortoise might be.

Key Features: Full control via custom code (Python), hosting for any open-source model, native support for Gradio and Streamlit UI frameworks, scalable compute resources (CPU/GPU), Git-based workflow for deployment.

Platform Availability: Development is done on Windows, macOS, or Linux; the final application is accessed via the Web.

26

Choose your tools! Tech Stacks

In the previous chapter we looked at individual tools and new viewpoints on how to utilize them. In this chapter we will take a step further and start talking about full "stacks" of tools to make a full solution, in this case, an end-to-end book creation to publication solution.

Combinations of tools get combined together to handle all the different parts of the process from creation of your manuscript all the way to publishing the book at the end. There are not right or wrong answers for how you do that, your own needs will dictate many of these decisions, but there's a lot of flexibility possible today that can help you address your individual needs whether you fall more into the strategist type of author or the technologist type.

Strategist vs. Technologist Architectures

Below are described two distinct, yet connected, publishing architectures defined by the choice of tooling and workflow. What's best for you might be completely different, but utilize this to get a feel for how all these tools can be pulled together to make a cohesive publishing chain.

The GUI/Service Architecture (The Strategist's Path):

This architecture prioritizes abstraction, speed-to-market, and purchasing solutions to complex problems. It relies on subscription-based services (ConvertKit, BookBub, Canva) and powerful GUI software (Scrivener, Vellum, Squarespace). Interoperability here relies on *vendor integrations* and standardized file formats (.docx, standard image files, and direct platform APIs).

The Code/FOSS Architecture (The Technologist's Path):

This architecture prioritizes control, long-term cost reduction, and scalability through automation. It is fundamentally built upon the **Pandoc** layer, using **Markdown** as the single source of truth for the manuscript. Interoperability relies on open-source standards, command-line interfaces, and APIs managed through orchestration tools like **n8n** and contained environments like **Docker**.

INTEGRATIONS AND CONVERSIONS:

When you use a combination of tools rather than just one vendors integrated option the challenge becomes how you can convert between them. What if they don't use the same formats? What if they are different cloud services that need to talk to each other? All of these things become considerations when you choose your tools.

1. **Editing Pipeline Bridge:** This is the most crucial hand-off. The Author-Strategist's feedback is usually delivered via tracked changes in **Google Docs** or **Microsoft Word**. The Author-Technologist uses **Pandoc** to convert that highly marked-up .docx file back into clean **Markdown** for version control in Git, or uses specialized tools like **Autocrit** and **ProWritingAid** which accept common input formats regardless of the author's drafting environment.

2. **Asset Pipeline Bridge:** **Canva**, **Affinity Publisher**, **GIMP**, and **Inkscape** produce standard binary files (PNG, JPEG, SVG, PDF/X-1a). These static assets are stored, often using **Git LFS**, and then

referenced by the Technologist's build tools (**Hugo**, **LaTeX**) for placement in the final website or manuscript.

- As a side note, keep in mind that these examples are just meant to give you ideas of what's possible. Git LFS is likely overkill for many projects, you would use it if you had a lot of large assets generated for your book.

3. **Automated Marketing Bridge:** Services like **ConvertKit** and **Book-Funnel** are necessary for platform reach. The Author-Technologist links these services to their custom infrastructure using an automation hub (**n8n**). For example, a successful checkout on **Gumroad** can trigger an API call to **n8n**, which then adds the buyer to a segmented list in **Listmonk**.

STRATEGIC TECH STACKS FOR SELF~PUBLISHING

The following stacks combine tools to form complete, functional systems tailored to each persona's strengths and goals, moving from reliable, common combinations to high-leverage, emerging architectural designs.

Author-Strategist Stacks

The focus here is minimizing cognitive load, maximizing professional output quality, and leveraging best-in-class subscription services for maximum marketing reach.

Stack Name	Goal and Key Tools	Workflow Architecture
Popular and Proven Combinations		

Stack Name	Goal and Key Tools	Workflow Architecture
1. The Frictionless Fiction Factory	Maximize speed-to-market and appearance with minimal effort.	Scrivener (Drafting), Google Docs (Editor), Vellum (Formatting), ConvertKit (List), Squarespace (Web)
2. The Advertising Funnel	Focus resources on acquisition channels and review accumulation.	Booksprout and NetGalley (ARC and Review), BookBub (Advertising), Publisher Rocket (Keywords), Mailchimp (Basic CRM)
3. Visual Non-Fiction Power	Handling complex interior design with robust commercial tools.	MS Word (Drafting/Collab), Affinity Publisher (Layout), Canva (Marketing Assets), Wix (Flexible Site Design)
4. Web Fiction to Print Strategy	Build audience through serialization before commercial release.	Royal Road (Audience Build), ProWritingAid (Self-Edit), BookFunnel (Magnet Delivery), Atticus (Cross-Platform Format)

Stack Name	Goal and Key Tools	Workflow Architecture
5. Project Management Overhead	Standardizing the production business.	Asana/Trello (Launch Management), Grammarly (Copywriting QA), Book Brush (Marketing Asset Gen)
Unique and Emerging Opportunities (High-Leverage)		
6. AI-Accelerated Content Engine	Use AI to drastically speed up idea generation and draft expansion.	Plottr (Structural Planning), Sudowrite (Co-Drafting), Autocrit (Initial QA), Vellum (Final Polish)
7. The Direct-to-Fan Audio Model	Bypass traditional audio distributors and capture maximum profit margin.	Manuscript (Drafting), ElevenLabs (AI Narration and Production), ConvertKit (Email List), Gumroad (Direct E-commerce Sales)
8. Immersive Branding System	Utilizing custom AI for deeper audience engagement.	Google AI Studio App Builder (Lore QA App), Squarespace (Host Embed), Pinterest (Visual Storyboarding)

Stack Name	Goal and Key Tools	Workflow Architecture
9. Podcast and Companion Strategy	Utilizing content strategy for book promotion.	Audacity (Recording/Editing), Miro (Episode Mapping), BookTok (Clip Marketing)
10. The Scalable Scaffolding Launch	Prioritize speed on initial website creation.	DeepSite (Website Template Gen), Canva (Asset Creation), Trello (Launch Task Management)

Author-Technologist Stacks

The focus here is on **Git**, automation, FOSS tools, complete control over data, and a reproducible build environment managed via code.

Stack Name	Goal & Key Tools	Workflow Architecture
Popular & Proven Combinations		
1. The Pure FOSS Production Chain	Minimal licensing cost and maximum system transparency.	Obsidian (Drafting/Notes), GIMP & Inkscape (Cover Art), Pandoc + LaTeX (Typesetting), Scribus (Print Layout Check)

Stack Name	Goal & Key Tools	Workflow Architecture
2. The Lean, Mean Website Machine	Utilizing standard FOSS web hosting for maximum performance.	Jekyll (Static Site Core), Git (Version Control), GitHub Pages (Free Hosting), LanguageTool (Content QA)
3. Academic/Technical Author Standard	Handling complex data structures and precise diagrams.	Obsidian (Structured Notes), Pandoc, Diagrams as Code (PlantUML), LaTeX (Final Output)
4. Professional Vector & Raster Master	High-end visual control using powerful FOSS tools.	Krita (Digital Painting), GIMP (Image Processing), Inkscape (Vector Elements)
5. DIY Mailing List Authority	Achieving bulk email service freedom and extreme cost savings.	Listmonk (Self-Hosted SMTP), StoryOrigin (List-Building Traffic)
Unique & Emerging Opportunities (High-Leverage)		
6. The Automated Build Factory	Using containerization to ensure platform parity and reproducibility.	Docker (Environment), Git (Orchestration), Pandoc (Automated Builds), Git LFS (Asset Storage)

Stack Name	Goal & Key Tools	Workflow Architecture
7. CI/CD Workflow Integration	Utilizing visual flow tools to manage automated production tasks.	Pandoc (Build Trigger), n8n (Automation Hub), BookFunnel API (Automated File Upload/Release),Asana (Task Completion Update)
8. Hyper-Specialized Web App Platform	Utilizing bespoke AI models for unique author applications.	Hugging Face Spaces (Docker Deployment), Affinity Publisher (Template Input), Gumroad API (License Integration)
9. Full AI Creative Loop	Integrating LLMs directly into the core writing process.	Sudowrite API (Generation Engine),Python Scripts (Draft Management), Obsidian (Note Sync/Local Storage)
10. Advanced Website Scaffold Refinement	Using AI for rapid deployment followed by expert refinement.	DeepSite (Code Gen Starter), Hugo (Fast Site Compiler), Dev Containers (Consistent Code Editor Setup)

27

PART 4: THE AI~POWERED AUTHOR

Welcome to the final section of the book. If the previous parts were about building your publishing system, this part is about upgrading it with a new power source. Here, we move beyond using off-the-shelf AI tools and into the realm of creating AI-driven solutions that are tailored to your specific needs as an author.

This is the "deep dive" section for the modern author. We will explore the next horizon of AI in publishing, from building a custom writing assistant that knows your voice to creating an AI-narrated audiobook or developing an AI-driven marketing engine.

The following chapters and workshops are designed to be both practical and forward-looking, giving you the tools and concepts you need to not just participate in the age of AI, but to thrive in it.

28

Custom AI Assistants: Fine~Tuning and RAG

Using a public AI model is powerful. Using an AI that has been trained on your own work and knows your world as well as you do is a superpower. This chapter explores the two primary methods for creating a bespoke AI assistant: **Retrieval-Augmented Generation (RAG)** and **Fine-Tuning**.

The Two Paths to a Custom AI

Retrieval-Augmented Generation (RAG): This is the most accessible method. You take a powerful, general purpose LLM and provide it with a "library" of your specific documents. When you ask a question, the AI first *retrieves* the most relevant passages from your library and then uses that information to *generate* its answer. It is an "open-book" exam for the AI.

Fine-Tuning: This is a more complex process where you take a base model and continue its training using your own dataset (e.g., your entire backlist of novels). The goal is to adjust the model's internal "weights" so that its very style, tone, and vocabulary begin to mimic your own. It is less about retrieving facts and more about learning a voice.

For most authors, RAG is the more practical and immediately useful technique.

THE STRATEGIST'S PATH: THE POWER OF NOTEBOOKLM

For the Author-Strategist, the goal is to get the power of a custom AI with the least amount of technical friction. The clear winner in this space is **Google NotebookLM**.

Based on extensive personal use for this and other book projects, I highly recommend NotebookLM as the starting point for any author. The process is simple:

1. Create a free Google account or use an existing one.

2. Log in to Google and find the applications list to find NotebookLM.

3. Create a new "notebook" for your project.

4. Upload your files: your full manuscript (as a PDF or Google Doc), character profiles, world building documents, research notes, and even web URLs.

5. Start asking questions.

That's it. You can immediately ask complex questions like, "What was the name of the tavern in Chapter 3, and did I ever describe its owner?" or "Summarize the key events of the protagonist's backstory." The AI will answer based *only* on the sources you provided, making it an incredibly powerful and accurate "lore keeper" for maintaining consistency in a complex series.

THE TECHNOLOGIST'S PATH: LOCAL RAG IN VS CODE

For the Author-Technologist who wants ultimate control and privacy, it is possible to run a RAG system entirely on your local machine, often directly within your code editor. VS Code extensions like **Roo Code** and **Continue** have built-in facilities for setting this up.

Based on my experience setting up both, I have settled on **Roo Code** as a powerful and effective tool. However, this path comes with significant challenges. Also, these extensions just have built in indexing rather than a true RAG solution, and it's using generic settings to break up the text of your project files. It works a lot better for software than for books as it doesn't tend to break up in the right spots to be helpful for context in later AI assisted questions.

- **The Embeddings Hurdle:** To make your documents searchable, they must be broken down into "chunks" and converted into numerical representations by an **embeddings model** and these chunks saved to a vector database. Setting up and managing this process is a technical step that can be a hurdle for new users. What makes it worse is default settings might just make standard size chunks which might break up things like chapters, in places that don't help for your context needs later when trying to use the index. Unless you go pretty deep into the details behind these systems, they are not simple to set up and require detailed understanding of how you will use them to be done properly. I'm not saying you shouldn't try if you are a technical person, just be aware that it's a full project on it's own that can easily distract from your book writing. You will need several other software components to bring this all together, locally you can use Qdrant or some other vector database, possibly a docker container to run Qdrant in, Ollama or one of the other tools that let you run local models, and an embeddings model to configure to be used when determining the chunks to store in the vector database. Many would use a paid service to do this work via api calls instead.

- **The Pace of Change:** These extensions evolve at a dizzying pace. An online tutorial or even AI generated setup advice can be outdated in a matter of weeks, as the version from "last week" may have a completely different interface or configuration process. You must be prepared for a certain amount of trial and error.

- **The Foam Advantage:** The power of a local RAG system is magnified when combined with a well structured notes repository. Using a tool like **Foam** to create explicit, hyperlinked connections between your notes ([[Character A]] is the brother of [[Character B]]) provides the RAG system with a rich, pre-built network of relationships to draw upon, leading to more insightful and accurate answers. Note that Using Foam when also using an extension to submit context is not directly related. Foam is useful for the same reasons RAG is, but more for when you are still building your book and want to find the relationships between characters and/or chapters.

Want to dive in?

Let's break down some learning options that were current at the time of writing this book. Some will still be fully relevant, but parts of this have been rapidly evolving to be better and better with less work. In a field that moves this quickly, it's crucial to periodically refresh and validate your learning resources. This goes way outside of the publishing space, but I include it here because if you are on the technologist's path, you might also be interested in the technology you'll be using to help you create many books.

The foundational sources will remain essential. The work of Jay Alammar is still the best starting point for intuition, and the original HNSW and RAG papers are still "must-reads" for understanding the core principles. The pace of innovation hasn't invalidated the fundamentals; it has built upon them.

However, the landscape *has* evolved. To be truly up-to-date, you need to add sources that cover the latest research, engineering best practices, and emergent trends.

Here is a specific, structured list of sources you can add directly to a NotebookLM instance to build a deep understanding from the ground up. This list is designed to take you through Phase 1 (Fundamentals) and Phase 2 (Algorithms) with a mix of intuitive explanations, technical deep dives, and original source material.

RAG Fundamentals (The "Why")

Your goal here is to be able to understand the core concepts and their implications.

Embeddings - From Words to Vectors

1. Video (Intuition): The Illustrated Word2Vec by Jay Alammar

   - **Source:** YouTube video titled "The Illustrated Word2vec, made easy" or the blog post "The Illustrated Word2Vec".

   - **Why:** This is an intuitive explanation of how the concept of turning words into meaningful vectors began. Understanding this provides the foundation for everything that follows.

2. Article (Modern Approach): The Illustrated Transformer by Jay Alammar

   - **Source:** Jay Alammar's Blog - `jalammar.github.io/illustrated-transformer/`

   - **Why:** This explains the architecture (attention, positional encoding) that powers modern models, which create the high-quality embeddings you use in RAG.

3. Documentation (Practical Application): Sentence-Transformers Documentation

   - **Source:** `sbert.net/docs/quickstart.html`

   - **Why:** This is the source documentation for the library most people use to generate embeddings. It bridges the theory of Transformers to the practical act of turning a sentence into a single vector for use in a vector database.

Distance Metrics - Measuring "Closeness"

1. Video (Core Concept): StatQuest: Cosine Similarity, Clearly Explained

   - **Source:** YouTube - Search for this exact title by StatQuest with Josh Starmer.

   - **Why:** Provides a simple, visual, and unforgettable explanation of the most common metric for text embeddings. You will never forget what it means after watching this.

2. Article (Practical Comparison): Vector Similarity Measures by Pinecone

   - **Source:** Pinecone's Blog - `pinecone.io/learn/vector-similarity/`

   - **Why:** This article is an excellent, concise comparison of the "big three": Cosine Similarity, Euclidean Distance (L2), and Dot Product. It explains the *when* and *why* for choosing each one in the context of vector search.

3. Reference (Comprehensive Overview): Scikit-learn: Distance Metrics Documentation

   - **Source:** `scikit-learn.org/stable/modules/ generated/ sklearn.metrics.pairwise.distance_metrics.html`

   - **Why:** Skim this page to see the sheer breadth of available metrics. You don't need to know them all, but it solidifies the idea that "distance" is a flexible, mathematically defined concept.

The Curse of Dimensionality

1. Article (Conceptual Understanding): What is the Curse of Dimensionality? by Kevin T. Keys

   - **Source:** Towards Data Science blog on Medium. `towards-datascience.com/` `the-curse-of-dimensionality-50dc6e49aa1e`

   - **Why:** This article provides a clear, non-intimidating explanation of *why* searching in high-dimensional space is so hard and why brute-force search is impossible at scale. This is the justification for all the algorithms in Phase 2.

Hybrid Search

1. Articles

   - **Source:** Weaviate Blog - Search for articles on "Hybrid Search".

   - **Why:** Combining traditional keyword search (sparse vectors, like BM25) with semantic vector search (dense vectors) is no longer an advanced technique; it's a standard practice for building robust retrieval systems. This can be required to handle keywords, product codes, and specific names that embeddings can miss, and is critical to how results are fused.

Dive into the Algorithms (The "How")

Your goal here is to understand the different strategies for finding *Approximate* Nearest Neighbors (ANN) and their trade-offs.

The Big Picture of ANN

1. Article (Landscape Overview): The Missing Readme: A Guide to Vector Databases by Pinecone

   - **Source:** `pinecone.io/learn/vector-database/`

   - **Why:** This guide gives a fantastic high-level overview of why vector databases are needed and introduces the main families of ANN algorithms you're about to study (graph-based, hashing, etc.).

Graph-Based Algorithms (HNSW) - The Industry Standard

1. Article (Intuitive Explanation): A Deep Dive on HNSW by Pinecone

   - **Source:** `pinecone.io/learn/hnsw/`

   - **Why:** This is the best place to start. It explains the intuition behind the multi-layer graph structure of HNSW without overwhelming you with math. **If you only read one algorithm article, make it this one.**

2. Paper (The Source): "Efficient and robust approximate nearest neighbor search using Hierarchical Navigable Small World graphs" by Malkov & Yashunin

   - **Source:** arXiv - `arxiv.org/abs/1603.09320`

   - **Why:** Add this to your notebook to study *after* you understand the intuitive explanation. Reading the abstract, introduction, and conclusion will give you the language and key contributions that you can reference in an interview.

3. Paper: "Three Algorithms for Merging Hierarchical Navigable Small World Graphs".

- **Source:** arXiv - `arxiv.org/abs/2505.16064`

- **Why:** HNSW is mature and current research is focused on operational challenges like efficiently merging indexes without rebuilding them from scratch, which is a critical task for distributed and real-time systems.

4. Article (Conceptual): "8-bit Rotational Quantization".

    - **Source:** Weaviate - `weaviate.io/blog/8-bit-rotational-quantization`

    - **Why:** The earlier Pinecone article is still good, but quantization research has advanced. Weaviate's work on Rotational Quantization (RQ) and other 8-bit techniques represents the state-of-the-art in compressing vectors to save memory and improve the speed/quality trade-off. Would this matter to your book project? Probably not, but again, if you are on the technologist path I'm trying not to to assume your projects don't need this level of detail.

5. Paper: "VQ-LLM: High-performance Code Generation for Vector Quantization Augmented LLM Inference".

    - **Source:** arXiv - `arxiv.org/abs/2503.02236`

    - **Why:** This connects vector database techniques directly to LLM inference optimization. It highlights that quantization isn't just for storage; it's a critical component for reducing memory traffic and latency on modern hardware (GPUs).

6. Paper: "BANG: Billion-Scale Approximate Nearest Neighbour Search using a Single GPU".

    - **Source:** arXiv - `https://arxiv.org/abs/2401.11324`

- **Why:** This paper addresses a key engineering challenge: how to handle datasets that are too large to fit entirely in GPU memory. It discusses the trade-offs between GPU and CPU memory access and showcases techniques for optimizing data transfer. I can't imagine any book project big enough to need to concern yourself with this, but I don't know the scale of what you are working on.

Quantization-Based Algorithms (PQ / ScaNN)

1. Article (Practical Explanation): "Scalar Quantization and Product Quantization" by Pinecone

   - **Source:** `pinecone.io/learn/product-quantization/`

   - **Why:** Explains the core idea of vector compression to save memory and increase speed. Understanding this is key to understanding how systems scale to billions of vectors.

2. Practical Guide (The Trade-offs): "FAISS Wiki: Guidelines to choose an index"

   - **Source:** `github.com/facebookresearch/faiss/ wiki/ Guidelines-to-choose-an-index`

   - **Why:** This is an amazing resource. It's a pragmatic guide from the creators of the most famous ANN library. It presents a flowchart that forces you to think about the trade-offs: "Do I need the absolute best accuracy? Is memory my main constraint? How fast does it need to be?" This will build your engineering mindset and help you choose what kind of system you might need for your use case.

Other Major Families (for Completeness)

1. Hashing-Based (LSH): "Locality Sensitive Hashing (LSH): The Illustrated Guide" by Pinecone.

   - **Source:** `pinecone.io/learn/series/faiss/locality-sensitive-hashing/`

   - **Why:** A widely popular technique used in approximate nearest neighbor (ANN) search. Similar items are more likely to end up in the same hash bucket.

2. Tree-Based (Annoy): Annoy GitHub Repository Readme

   - **Source:** `github.com/spotify/annoy`

   - **Why:** The creator of Annoy (Erik Bernhardsson) explains its core logic right on the front page. It's a simple, elegant explanation of how tree-based partitioning of the vector space works.

PUTTING IT ALL TOGETHER

The entire field of vector search is being driven by the needs of Retrieval-Augmented Generation (RAG). Understanding these algorithms helps you see how they improve the retrieval step of a RAG pipeline.

The core algorithm is stable and dominant. The interesting work is now in operational efficiency: merging, updating, and distributing HNSW graphs.

As vector datasets grow into the billions and trillions, naive storage of full-precision vectors is no longer feasible. Quantization techniques like PQ, RQ, etc. are possible solutions that can have a big impact on hardware performance.

A pure vector search solution is often not enough on it's own. You may need to build a hybrid search option that blends keyword and semantic search.

If you read through the core papers and articles you'll have a working knowledge of how RAG works and likely you'll be able to know how appropriate it is for your book project. Once you read through these, if you do implement some form of RAG I recommend you add the items related to what you use to a NotebookLM notebook. This is immensely helpful to ask questions that will get you much more focused answers than a web search.

29

Audio: AI Voice Cloning and Audiobook Production

For decades, the high cost of professional narration and studio time has made audiobook production an insurmountable barrier for many independent authors. That barrier has been completely demolished by the rise of high fidelity, AI powered text-to-speech platforms.

This chapter provides a deep dive into this revolutionary technology, offering a practical workflow for turning your manuscript into a professional quality audiobook for a fraction of the traditional cost.

The Technology: Voice Cloning and Synthesis

The leading platform in this space is **ElevenLabs**. The quality of its synthesized voices is now virtually indistinguishable from human narration for a well prepared text. The platform allows you to either use one of its premade, professional voices or to "clone" your own voice from a few minutes of sample audio.

A Note on Ethics: Cloning your own voice is a powerful branding tool. Cloning someone else's voice without their explicit, enthusiastic consent is an ethical and legal minefield. This guide assumes you will only be cloning your own voice or using the pre-made voices provided by the service.

The Business Case: A Real World Example

The barrier to entry is now incredibly low. Based on direct experience creating audio with ElevenLabs for a separate project, the platform's free tier provides approximately 10,000 generation credits. This is enough to produce roughly one full length chapter, making it a perfect, no cost method to create a "pilot episode" to validate the quality and process.

To produce a full length novel, a subscription is required, but the cost is a tiny fraction of the thousands of dollars required for traditional audiobook production, making the return on investment highly favorable for indie authors.

The Workflow: From Text to Audiobook

1. **Text Preparation (The Most Critical Step):** AI narrators are literal. They will read exactly what they see. Before you generate any audio, you must perform a "narration pass" on your manuscript.

   - Spell out numbers: "1984" should become "nineteen eighty-four."

   - Use phonetic spellings for unusual names or words.

   - For advanced control, learn the basics of **Speech Synthesis Markup Language (SSML)**. This simple markup allows you to insert specific pauses (`<break time="1s"/>`) or change emphasis, giving you director-level control over the final performance.

2. **Voice Selection or Cloning:**

   - **Pre-made Voice:** Select a stock voice from the platform's library that fits the tone and genre of your book.

- **Voice Cloning:** Follow the platform's instructions to record samples of your own voice. The more varied your intonation during the recording, the more flexible your cloned voice will be.

3. **Chapter by Chapter Generation:** Do not try to generate your entire book at once. Render the audio one chapter at a time. This makes it easier to manage the files, correct any errors, and make minor edits to the text as you go.

4. **Assembly and Mastering:**

   - Use a free audio editor like **Audacity** to assemble your generated chapter files into a single audio track.

   - Add opening and closing credits.

   - Use Audacity's tools to master the audio to meet the specific technical requirements (e.g., RMS levels, peak volume, noise floor) for your chosen distribution platform, such as Audible's **ACX**.

By following this workflow, you can create a new, highly valuable version of your book and open up a significant new revenue stream that was previously out of reach for most authors.

As a professional voice actor with a high degree of technical expertise, you are in a prime position to leverage the power of cutting-edge text-to-speech (TTS) and voice cloning technologies. These tools can augment your workflow, open up new creative avenues, and even create new revenue streams. Here's a comprehensive breakdown of Tortoise TTS, Eleven Labs, and Chatterbox, along with other notable tools, to help you navigate this evolving landscape.

Voice Options

Just to go a little bit deeper than the main workflow, below is a more detailed look. Keep in mind there is another view of some of these in the tools section, but this is meant to dive into the primary self publishing author options when you don't want to hire a professional firm to create your marketing materials and audio books.

Tortoise TTS: This is a powerful, open-source TTS model known for its high quality, natural sounding speech and impressive voice cloning capabilities, often requiring only a few short audio samples. Its name, "Tortoise," playfully alludes to its slower processing speed, a trade off for its remarkable quality. Being open source, it offers a high degree of flexibility and customization for those with the technical skills to modify and train the model.

Eleven Labs: A commercially focused platform that has gained significant traction for its incredibly realistic and emotionally expressive AI voices. It offers a user friendly interface, a wide range of pre-existing voices, and robust voice cloning features. Eleven Labs is designed for ease of use and rapid content production, making it a popular choice for creators and businesses. They have also expanded into a full audiobook creation and publishing platform.

Chatterbox: A newer, open-source TTS model from Resemble AI that has quickly gained attention for its impressive voice cloning from very short audio samples (as little as 5 seconds) and its unique emotion control features. It positions itself as a strong, free alternative to commercial platforms like Eleven Labs, with blind tests suggesting a user preference for its realism and emotional depth in some cases.

Side~by~Side Comparison for the Technically Minded Author

Here is a detailed comparison to help you decide which tool best suits your needs:

Capability	Tortoise TTS	Eleven Labs	Chatterbox
Primary Use Case	High quality, personalized voice synthesis for those with technical expertise.	Professional grade voice generation, voice cloning, and audiobook creation for creators and businesses.	Open source, real time voice synthesis with a focus on emotional control and rapid voice cloning.
Voice Cloning	Excellent. Can replicate voices from a few short audio clips (e.g., 3-5 clips of 10 seconds each).	Excellent. Offers Instant Voice Cloning from short samples and "Professional Voice Cloning" for higher fidelity.	Excellent. Zero-shot voice cloning from as little as a 5-second audio sample.
Emotional Range	Highly realistic prosody and intonation, but less direct control over specific emotions.	High. Known for its ability to generate speech with a wide range of emotions and contextual awareness.	High. A key feature is its "exaggeration control" slider, allowing for fine-tuning of emotional intensity.

Capability	Tortoise TTS	Eleven Labs	Chatterbox
Ease of Use	Difficult. Requires significant technical knowledge to set up and use effectively. Often requires working with code and command-line interfaces.	Easy. User friendly web interface and API access.	Moderate to Difficult. While a demo is available, full implementation requires technical expertise.
Customization	Very High. As an open source model, you can fine-tune it with your own data for specific vocal styles.	Moderate. Offers adjustments for pitch, tone, and pacing. Custom voice creation is a core feature.	High. Being open-source allows for deep customization for those with the right skills.
Speed	Slow. The name reflects its deliberate pace in generating high quality audio.	Fast. Optimized for quick and efficient speech generation, with a low-latency "Turbo" model available.	Very Fast. Claims sub-200ms latency, making it suitable for real time applications.

Capability	Tortoise TTS	Eleven Labs	Chatterbox
Language Support	Limited compared to commercial offerings.	Extensive. Supports over 70 languages and various accents.	Primarily focused on English, but with multilingual capabilities that can be expanded by the community.
Cost	Free (Open Source). However, there are costs associated with the necessary computing power (GPU).	Paid subscription model with a free tier. Pricing scales with usage.	Free (Open Source).
Licensing	Open Source (MIT License). You can freely use and modify the code.	Proprietary, commercial license.	Open-Source (MIT License).
API Access	Yes, for programmatic use.	Yes, a robust API is a key feature for integration into other applications.	Yes, with Python API and other integrations.

Capability	Tortoise TTS	Eleven Labs	Chatterbox
Audiobook Specific Features	Not specifically designed for audiobooks, but can be used to generate the audio.	Yes, a dedicated audiobook creation and publishing platform with features for multi-character narration and chapter segmentation.	Can be used for audiobook generation, with examples of workflows available.

OTHER TOOLS TO CONSIDER FOR AUDIOBOOK CREATION

Beyond these three, the landscape of AI voice tools is rich and varied. Here are other platforms to keep on your radar.

- **Murf.ai:** Offers a suite of tools for creating voiceovers for various types of content, with options for adjusting pitch, speed, and emphasis.

- **Play.ht:** Boasts a large library of voices and languages and offers integrations with publishing platforms.

- **LOVO AI (Genny):** Provides realistic voices with an intuitive interface and built-in sound editing and mastering tools.

- **Descript:** An all-in-one audio and video editor with a feature called "Overdub" that allows you to create a text-to-speech model of your own voice.

- **Respeecher:** A high-end voice cloning tool often used in the film and television industry for creating seamless voice performances.

- **Speechify:** Known for its natural-sounding voices and a tool that can create simple video presentations with voiceovers.

- **WellSaid Labs:** Focuses on creating very high-quality, professional-sounding AI voices for corporate and commercial use.

The key is to view these tools not as replacements, but as powerful additions to your toolkit. They can be used for pre-visualization, creating placeholder audio, generating voices for background characters, or even for creating entirely new vocal performances under your direction. By understanding the capabilities and limitations of each, you can make an informed decision that aligns with your technical skills and creative goals.

30

AI for Marketing and Audience Growth: A Practical Guide

Marketing is often the most dreaded part of the self publishing journey. It can feel like a relentless, time consuming chore. However, by leveraging AI as a strategic partner, you can transform your marketing from a series of disjointed tasks into a powerful, automated system for audience growth.

This chapter focuses on practical, AI driven strategies that go beyond simple "write a tweet" prompts.

The Market Analysis Engine

Before you can market your book, you must understand the market. You can use a powerful LLM with web-browsing capabilities to act as your personal market research analyst.

Example Prompt:

> "Act as a professional book market analyst. My book is a [Your Genre]. I want you to analyze the top 10 bestselling books in this category on Amazon right now. Provide me with a report that identifies:

1. Common trends in cover design (e.g., color palettes, imagery, typography).

2. Common themes and tropes mentioned in the book descriptions.

3. The average price point for ebooks and paperbacks in this category."

This prompt gives you a high-level overview of reader expectations in your genre in minutes, a task that would have once taken hours of manual research.

The Content Generation Engine

One of the biggest marketing challenges is the constant need for new content. You can use AI to create a virtually endless supply of on-brand ideas.

Example Prompt:

"Act as my social media marketing manager. I am providing you with the synopsis and key themes of my book below. Your task is to generate a one-month social media content calendar.

For each week, provide me with:

- Two thought-provoking questions to ask my audience.

- Two interesting facts related to my book's themes.

- One idea for a short blog post or newsletter article.

[Paste your book's synopsis and list of themes here]"

This turns the AI into a tireless brainstorming partner, freeing you up to focus on writing and engaging with your readers.

The Ad Copy Factory (A/B Testing)

Writing effective ad copy is difficult. AI can help you rapidly test different angles to see what resonates with readers.

Example Prompt:

"Act as an expert direct-response copywriter specializing in Amazon Ads. My book is a [Your Genre] about [Your Synopsis].

Your task is to write five different ad headlines for my book. Each headline should focus on a different emotional hook:

1. One focused on mystery and intrigue.
2. One focused on action and excitement.
3. One focused on the main character's internal conflict.
4. One focused on the high stakes of the plot.
5. One that asks a compelling question."

You can then run small, targeted ad campaigns with each headline to see which one gets the most clicks, providing you with real-world data on what marketing message is most effective.

The Personalized Email Marketing Assistant

You can use AI to draft tailored email sequences for different segments of your audience, making your marketing more personal and effective.

Example Prompt:

> "Act as my email marketing manager. I need to write a 3-part automated email sequence for readers who have just finished Book 1 of my series and whom I want to encourage to buy Book 2.

> - **Email 1:** A 'thank you' for reading Book 1 that hints at the unresolved plot threads.
> - **Email 2:** A 'behind-the-scenes' look at a favorite character from Book 1 who plays a major role in Book 2.
> - **Email 3:** A direct call to action to buy Book 2, with a clear link and a compelling, spoiler-free hook."

By using AI as a strategic marketing partner, you can build a powerful system for reaching new readers and engaging your existing fans, all while saving yourself hundreds of hours of work.

31

PROMPT ENGINEERING WORKSHOP

The Art and Science of Conversation

Welcome to the single most important skill for leveraging AI: **prompt engineering**. This isn't a technical coding skill; it's the art and science of having a clear, effective conversation with an incredibly powerful assistant. A weak prompt leads to a weak result. A great prompt can produce professional grade work in seconds.

This workshop will teach you how to move from simple questions to sophisticated instructions, empowering you to get the most out of any Large Language Model (LLM) you use.

THE FOUR TYPES OF PROMPTS FOR AUTHORS

Most requests you make of an AI will fall into one of four categories. Understanding them gives you a mental model for your own work.

The "Brainstorming" Prompt:

Used for generating raw ideas and possibilities. This is a low-stakes, high-creativity prompt.

Prompt Example:

> "Give me ten potential titles for a fantasy novel about a librarian who discovers a book that writes itself."

The "Persona" Prompt:

The most powerful type. You assign the AI a role or a character, which dramatically improves the quality and focus of its response.

Prompt Example:

> "Act as an expert book copywriter. Your task is to write a compelling blurb for my new thriller."

The "Stylistic Transformation" Prompt:

Used for taking existing text and changing it.

Prompt Example:

> "Rewrite the following paragraph in a more exciting and suspenseful tone," or "Summarize this chapter into three bullet points."

The "Structured Output" Prompt:

Used when you need the AI to return information in a specific, predictable format.

Prompt Example:

"Analyze the following text and provide a list of the main characters in a JSON format with 'name' and 'motivation' as keys."

THE CORE PRINCIPLES OF EFFECTIVE PROMPTING

Provide Context:

The more background information the AI has, the better its output. A prompt that includes your book's synopsis, genre, and target audience will always outperform one that doesn't.

Assign a Role (The Persona):

Always start your prompt by telling the AI *who* it is. "Act as a..." is the most powerful phrase in prompt engineering.

Be Specific and Clear:

Avoid ambiguity. Instead of "Write a blurb," use "Write a 150-word blurb with a strong hook, targeting fans of military sci-fi."

Use Constraints:

Tell the AI what *not* to do. This is a powerful way to refine the output. Examples: "Do not use clichés," "Avoid passive voice," "The tone should be professional, not casual."

Know Your Model (A Brief Guide)

The AI landscape is dominated by a few key players and this is rapidly evolving. While the underlying principles of prompting are universal, each model has a slightly different "personality." Each new model that comes out improves on performance, but also changes the equation of what prompting works best.

Regardless of whether a model is known for being good at a task or not, keep in mind that you must be using prompting styles that work with the way that model was trained and that is not always obvious.

OpenAI's GPT Series:

Often considered the most creative and better for writing of the models. Excellent for brainstorming, drafting prose, and complex reasoning. However, your own style and ability at prompting is more likely to determine what kind of results you get.

Google's Gemini Family:

Known for its deep integration with Google's search index, making it incredibly powerful for research-based tasks and factual accuracy. I personally have had excellent success using Gemini models to assist with writing.

Anthropic's Claude Family:

Often praised for its ability to handle very large amounts of text (a large "context window") and for its more conversational, collaborative tone.

Others:

There are many, many more, I won't try to make an exhaustive list here, grok for example is another highly rated one. But don't worry too much about knowing all the models, try some and start to get a feel for what you want to do with them.

The prompt that works perfectly in one model may need adjustments for another. The best practice is to be flexible and willing to adapt your wording.

When you hear the term "context window", there is really a lot behind the scenes for this, some models promote large context windows of 1 million or more, but there's also a max output context for models that can affect you as well, particularly if you tend to generate large outputs you can easily hit this limit even if you aren't even close to the overall published limit. There are many ways to handle this, but for the author just be aware of this as it's sometimes not obvious. If you are technically minded you can use your favorite LLM to dig in to how to solve the problem.

These limits are much more noticeable if you try to use local models as many of the free open source models have small context windows. This means that if you want to have assistance from a model to work on your book you might not be able to get enough of your text into the context being considered to answer your questions.

THE INTERACTIVE WORKFLOW: REFINING YOUR PROMPTS

A great prompt is rarely written on the first try. It's developed through an iterative conversation with your LLM of choice. Each model will have their own idiosyncrasies to be considered so you need to be specific about which one you are developing the model for. I mention this because many of the tools in this book use specific models that might be different than the one you use day-to-day.

Start Simple:

Write a basic prompt with a clear goal.

Analyze and Critique:

Look at the AI's response. What's good? What's missing? Is the tone right?

Refine and Add Detail:

Modify your prompt. Add more context from your creative brief, assign a stronger persona, or add a specific constraint.

Provide an Example ("Few-Shot" Prompting):

If you need a specific format, show the AI exactly what you want. For example: `Here is an example of a good tweet: [Example]. Now, write three similar tweets for my book.`

Chain Your Prompts:

Use the output of one prompt as the input for the next. This is how you create a powerful workflow, as demonstrated in the "AI Simulated Workshops" throughout this book.

Go to the Source

The companies that build these models want you to get good results. They all publish detailed guides on how to write effective prompts for their specific systems. These are the best and most up-to-date resources available.

To find them, simply search for:

- "OpenAI Prompting Guide"
- "Google Gemini Prompting Best Practices"

- "Anthropic Claude Prompting Resources"

Advanced Technique 1: The "Simulation Prompt"

This is the technique used to generate the "AI Simulated Workshops" in this book. It involves combining all the core principles into a single, comprehensive prompt that asks the AI to perform a complex, multi-step task while adopting a specific persona. It is the ultimate expression of treating the AI as a creative partner.

Key Components of a Simulation Prompt:

1. A clear, expert Persona.

2. A high-level Goal

3. A numbered list of specific Tasks to complete.

4. All the necessary Context (like a creative brief) pasted directly into the prompt.

Advanced Technique 2: The "System Prompt"

Some models support the use of system prompts. System prompts are provided to a model along with whatever prompt the user writes. You can take advantage of this to do things like direct the LLM on default personas, how you want to see your outputs, and many others. Below is the system prompt I developed while working on this book and for various other creative endeavors. I found this to be effective enough that I sent a copy of it to myself to use at my day job working in technology, and all I needed to change was the default personas to immediately get great results.

I encourage you to consider developing one of these through the iterative process described earlier that is specific to your own way of thinking.

Example Prompt:

"Phase 1: Framing & Planning (Setting the Context)

1. Unless the user's explicit persona or request suggests otherwise (e.g., 'explain this to me like I'm a beginner'), by default act as a Creative Systems Architect. Your expertise is in analyzing complex creative domains (like music production, art, linux based tools, writing, software development, self-publishing, desktop publishing, and digital media) as interconnected systems. You identify the essential components, workflows, and toolchains. Your goal is to find the optimal balance between creative quality, cost, and time-to-market for a solo creator or small team. You evaluate trade-offs, identify high-leverage steps, and spot workflow bottlenecks. You are technology-agnostic but favor solutions that are powerful, flexible, and efficient.

2. At the beginning of a complex analysis, consider stating any core assumptions made in a brief 'Assumptions' block (e.g., 'Assuming a cloud-native deployment model on Kubernetes...').

3. For highly complex, multi-faceted, or ambiguous requests, the model may optionally print a brief 'Research Strategy' before executing tool calls. This should be a 1-2 sentence statement outlining the key concepts it intends to investigate to ensure a comprehensive answer.

Phase 2: Core Analytical Mandates (The Heavy Lifting)

4. When evaluating options, conduct a scenario-based trade-off analysis. Frame the evaluation around distinct architectural goals (e.g., 'Speed-to-Market for a Startup', 'Scalability & Compliance for an Enterprise', 'Minimal Operational Overhead for a Solo Developer'). Use a matrix or narrative comparison to highlight how the best choice changes with context.

5. Where relevant and valuable, include a brief subsection on 'Common Anti-Patterns' or 'Second-Order Effects.' This should highlight common pitfalls, hidden costs, or downstream organizational/technical consequences associated with a particular architectural choice.

Phase 3: Output Structuring & Synthesis (Presenting the Analysis)

6. Begin with high-impact, actionable insights, followed by optional deeper context.

7. Use structured formats (e.g. bullet points, tables, decision matrices) unless a narrative is explicitly requested.

8. Where a complex system, process, or architectural relationship is described, consider suggesting a textual representation of a diagram (e.g., using Markdown, or pseudo-code like Service A -> [API Gateway] -> Service B) to visually clarify the concept for the user.

9. Conclude every response with a 'Strategic Synthesis' or 'Architect's View' section. In this section, move beyond the direct data and answer the 'so what?' question.

Synthesize the findings to offer a forward-looking opinion, identify non-obvious connections between trends, propose a novel architectural pattern based on the evidence, or highlight critical unanswered questions and emerging frontiers in the space.

Phase 4: Nuance & Style (The Final Polish)

10. Use precise, concise language, avoid filler or vague phrasing.

11. Avoid speculative or redundant content unless it clarifies uncertainty or informs strategic choices.

12. When discussing emerging frontiers or potential anti-patterns, use nuanced language to signal confidence levels (e.g., 'a likely outcome,' 'a plausible but unproven risk,' 'a high-confidence prediction based on current trajectories'). This avoids overstating speculative points and adds to the persona's realism.

Phase 5: Foundational Rules (Always-On Constraints)

13. When settings allow, always use a live search to get more up to date answers.

14. Ground all factual claims in the browsed results. Attribute sources at the end of the relevant paragraph or section using a consolidated reference (e.g., [1, 3]). Synthesized insights in the 'Strategic Synthesis' section do not require a direct citation but should be logically derived from the preceding evidence."

I strongly advise you to work with an LLM iteratively to come up with the best prompt for you. Also, be aware that some of these system prompt items can limit responses and might not be what you want for any given question. There are plenty of times where I won't want an analytical response but rather a more creative one and might only use part of this system prompt. It's all about getting the outputs as close as possible to your own style, and that takes a lot of back and forth with an LLM to narrow down what your responses will look like.

There are lots of detailed resources available related to prompt engineering and the space changes so rapidly that I would definitely be sure to do some digging to see specialized resources for better prompts.

32

Understanding LLM Parameters

Many AI tools have a selection of parameters that can be controlled to change the way the model reacts to your questions. I'll cover more of these momentarily, but the most easy to adjust parameter related to creative writing is the "temperature" setting. This is a simple, non-technical way to control the AI's creativity.

- **Low Temperature (e.g., 0.2):** This makes the AI more focused, predictable, and deterministic. It's good for factual tasks, summarization, and when you need a reliable, consistent output.

- **High Temperature (e.g., 1.0 or higher):** This makes the AI more random, creative, and surprising. It's excellent for brainstorming and generating multiple diverse ideas, but it is less reliable for following specific, detailed instructions.

Think of it as a "creativity" knob. Turn it down for precision, turn it up for inspiration.

Understanding the various "levers and controls" for Large Language Models (LLMs) allows you to precisely steer their behavior and output, much like adjusting faders and EQ on an audio mixer. These parameters directly influence creativity, coherence, length, and style.

The Deeper Look

You could stop just with understanding temperature if you do not want to get into the technical details. However, for the author-technologist, here is a breakdown of other parameters to be aware of. Keep in mind that each model might only expose one, three, or none of these, it's different with each provider and from model to model.

Core Generation parameters

Core Generation parameters influence the *randomness* and *diversity* of the generated text.

Temperature:

- **Description:** Like we mentioned above, temperature is a value that controls the randomness of the output. Higher values lead to more creative, diverse, and surprising text, while lower values make the output more deterministic, focused, and conservative.

- **Impact:**
  - **0.0 (or very low):** The model will always pick the most probable next token, resulting in highly predictable, often repetitive, and factual output. Good for strict summarization or code generation.
  - **0.7-1.0 (or higher):** The model considers a wider range of tokens, increasing creativity and variety. Good for brainstorming, creative writing, or generating diverse responses.

- **Analogy:** A "creativity dial."

Top-P (Nucleus Sampling):

- **Description:** A float value (typically 0.0 to 1.0) that determines the cumulative probability threshold for token selection. The model considers only the smallest set of most probable tokens whose cumulative probability exceeds p.

- **Impact:**

  - **0.0 (or very low):** Similar to low temperature, very restrictive.

  - **0.9-1.0:** Allows for a broader selection of tokens while still discarding very unlikely ones. Often used as an alternative or alongside temperature to control diversity.

- **Analogy:** A "probability budget" for token choices. If you have a higher number you are more likely to see items that are diverse.

Top-K:

- **Description:** An integer value that limits the model's choice to the K most probable next tokens.

- **Impact:**

  - **Low K:** Restricts the model to a very small set of highly probable tokens, making the output more focused and less varied.

  - **High K:** Allows for more diversity, but still limits the total pool of possible tokens.

- **Relationship to Top-P:** Top-P is generally preferred over Top-K because it dynamically adjusts the number of tokens based on their probability distribution, whereas Top-K is a fixed number.

Max Tokens or Max Length:

- **Description:** An integer that sets the maximum number of tokens the model will generate in its response. We mentioned this in the context of the context windows earlier in this book, max tokens is often confused with output max tokens.

- **Impact:** Directly controls the length of the output. Crucial for managing costs (as you pay per token) and ensuring responses are concise or fit within a specific format. Many models charge more for output tokens than input context tokens.

- **Note:** This is the *output* length; the *total* length of input + output is limited by the model's context window.

OUTPUT SHAPING PARAMETERS

These influence the *content* and *style* of the generated text, often preventing repetition.

Frequency Penalty:

- **Description:** A float value (typically 0.0 to 2.0) that reduces the likelihood of the model generating tokens that have *already appeared* in the response.

- **Impact:** Encourages the model to use a wider vocabulary and avoid repeating specific words or phrases.

- **Analogy:** "Word-specific anti-repetition."

Presence Penalty:

- **Description:** A float value (typically 0.0 to 2.0) that reduces the likelihood of the model generating *any token* that has *already been present* in the response.

- **Impact:** Encourages the model to introduce new topics or concepts and broaden its scope, rather than dwelling on what's already been mentioned.

- **Difference from Frequency:** Presence penalty cares if a token has *ever* appeared; Frequency penalty cares about *how often* it has appeared.

- **Analogy:** "Topic-specific novelty encouragement."

Stop Sequences:

- **Description:** A list of one or more strings of characters. If any of these strings are generated by the LLM, the output is immediately truncated at that point.

- **Impact:** Essential for structured output. For example, you can tell the model to stop generating when it encounters some specific string of characters or a closing JSON tag.

- **Analogy:** A "cut-off signal."

INPUT AND CONTEXT CONTROLS

These govern what the model perceives and how it interprets its task.

System Prompt / Instructions:

- **Description:** The initial text provided to the LLM that sets its persona, defines the task, outlines constraints, and provides context for the entire interaction.

- **Impact:** Fundamentally shapes the model's behavior, tone, and adherence to rules. "You are a helpful assistant." "Act as a professional voice director." "Generate a 50-word synopsis."

- **Analogy:** The "director's brief" or "character description."

Context Window (Implicit Control):

- **Description:** Not a direct parameter you set for *generation*, but an inherent limit of the specific LLM model being used. It's the total number of tokens (input prompt + previous turns in a conversation + generated output) the model can "see" and process at one time.

- **Impact:** Determines how long conversations can be, how much reference material can be provided, and the maximum complexity of tasks the model can handle within a single interaction.

- **Analogy:** The "RAM" or "short-term memory" of the model.

STRATEGIC APPROACHES (BEYOND DIRECT PARAMETERS)

Thinking vs. Coding (Chain-of-Thought Prompting):

- **Description:** This isn't a *parameter* but a *prompting strategy*. Instead of asking the LLM for a direct answer, you instruct it to "think step-by-step," "show its work," or "reason out loud" before arriving at a final conclusion.

- **Impact:** Significantly improves the accuracy and reliability of answers for complex reasoning tasks (math, logic puzzles, multi-step instructions, coding). By forcing the LLM to articulate its intermediate steps, it reduces the chance of logical errors or "hallucinations."

- **How to achieve:** Include phrases like "Let's think step by step," "Explain your reasoning," or structure your prompt to ask for intermediate steps explicitly.

- **Analogy:** Asking a student to "show their work" rather than just providing the answer.

Model Choice (Implicit Control):

- **Description:** The specific underlying LLM you choose (e.g., Gemini 2.5 pro, GPT-5, Claude, Llama, Mistral, etc.).

- **Impact:** This is perhaps the *biggest* lever. Different models have varying levels of intelligence, reasoning ability, knowledge, token limits, speed, and cost. Choosing a more capable model (like the latest version of GPT or Gemini) will fundamentally alter the quality and complexity of tasks it can handle, regardless of other parameters.

- **Analogy:** Choosing between a vintage condenser mic vs. a modern digital one – different core capabilities and inherent characteristics.

By mastering these controls, you can fine-tune LLM outputs to meet precise requirements, whether you're generating creative scripts, factual summaries, code, or even guiding an AI voice to emulate nuanced speech patterns.

Thinking Models

A "thinking model" isn't a distinct type of LLM, but rather a *strategic mode of operation* you elicit through specific prompting techniques. It's the process of compelling an LLM to move beyond providing a fast, reflexive answer and instead engage in a structured, deliberate reasoning process. You are essentially asking the model to "show its work" before delivering a conclusion.

This approach is based on the discovery that LLMs produce far more accurate and reliable results for complex tasks when they are forced to articulate their intermediate reasoning steps. By breaking a problem down and generating a "chain of thought," the model constrains itself to a logical path, dramatically reducing the likelihood of errors and hallucinations.

Think of it as the difference between an instinctual reaction and a carefully considered strategic plan.

When you see a model promoted as a thinking model, it means that it was trained on data to be optimized for the thinking style prompting noted above.

Core Purpose and Functionality

The primary purpose of employing a thinking model strategy is to unlock an LLM's capacity for advanced cognitive tasks that require logic, planning, and synthesis. Its key functions include:

- **Complex Reasoning:** Solving multi-step math problems, logic puzzles, and scientific questions where the answer isn't immediately obvious.

- **Strategic Planning:** Developing comprehensive business plans, marketing strategies, project outlines, or complex event schedules from a simple goal.

- **Data Synthesis and Analysis:** Reading and interpreting large volumes of text (e.g., multiple research papers, customer reviews, legal documents), identifying underlying themes, finding contradictions, and generating a coherent summary or analysis.

- **Creative Ideation:** Brainstorming complex narratives for a book or film, outlining character arcs, and ensuring plot points connect logically across a long story.

- **Critical Evaluation and Red Teaming:** Analyzing an argument, identifying its logical fallacies, proposing counter-arguments, and stress-testing a plan by identifying potential weaknesses or failure points.

Key Levers and Prompting Strategies for Thinking

Controlling a thinking model is less about tweaking parameters like temperature and more about architecting your prompt to build a "cognitive scaffold" for the model to work within.

Chain-of-Thought (CoT) Prompting (The Foundational Technique):

- **Description:** This is the most fundamental lever. You explicitly instruct the model to think before answering.

- **How to Apply:** Add simple phrases like *"Let's think step-by-step,"* *"Break this problem down first,"* or *"Show your reasoning before giving the final answer."*

- **Impact:** This simple instruction dramatically shifts the model's process. Instead of jumping to a conclusion, it generates a sequence of logical steps, which you can inspect and which guides the model to a more accurate final result.

Persona and Role Assignment (The "Expert"):

- **Description:** You assign the LLM a specific expert role. This grounds its reasoning process within the mental models and priorities of that profession.

- **How to Apply:** Begin your prompt with *"Act as a seasoned management consultant," "You are a skeptical investigative journalist,"* or *"Embody the role of a meticulous historian."*

- **Impact:** This goes beyond tone. A "consultant" will structure its thinking around frameworks like SWOT analysis. A "journalist" will focus on verifying facts and questioning assumptions. A "historian" will consider context and causality. This frames *how* it thinks.

Deconstruction and Synthesis (The "Divide and Conquer" Method):

- **Description:** For very large or ambiguous tasks, you guide the model to first break the problem into smaller, distinct sub-questions, answer each one methodically, and then synthesize the results into a final, cohesive answer.

- **How to Apply:** *"I need a report on the impact of AI on the film industry. First, create a list of key areas to investigate (e.g., pre-production, visual effects, marketing). Next, analyze the impact on each of those areas one by one. Finally, synthesize your findings into a comprehensive executive summary."*

- **Impact:** This prevents the model from getting lost or providing a superficial overview. It ensures a thorough, well-structured, and comprehensive output for complex analytical tasks.

Self-Correction and Critique (The "Internal Review"):

- **Description:** This is a powerful technique where you instruct the model to not only generate a plan or answer but also to critique its own output.

- **How to Apply:** After the model provides its step-by-step reasoning, your follow-up prompt could be: *"That's a good start. Now, review your own plan. What are its three biggest weaknesses? How could you mitigate them?"*

- **Impact:** This forces a deeper level of analysis and refinement. The model becomes its own "red team," identifying and patching holes in its logic, leading to a much more robust and defensible final output.

Tree of Thoughts (ToT) / Multi-Path Reasoning (The "Brainstorming" Method):

- **Description:** This is an advanced strategy where you prompt the model to explore multiple different reasoning paths or solutions to a problem in parallel, evaluate the pros and cons of each path, and then select or synthesize the best one.

- **How to Apply:** *"Propose three distinct strategies for launching a new podcast. For each strategy, outline the steps, the potential risks, and the likely outcomes. Finally, recommend the best strategy and justify your choice."*

- **Impact:** This prevents the model from settling on the first plausible solution it finds. It encourages divergent thinking and leads to more creative, resilient, and well-considered solutions.

Controlling the Final Output

After the extensive "thinking" process, it's crucial to get a clean, usable result. A key lever here is **output structuring**. End your prompt with a clear instruction on how to present the final answer, such as:

> *"After you have completed your step-by-step analysis, provide a final, concise answer inside a code block."*

This cleanly separates the messy but valuable reasoning process from the polished deliverable, allowing you to benefit from the former while using the latter.

I have found that there is no one right method that works for all situations, you really have to try this and keep trying other methods until you get a feel for what you like. I often find that using a combination of techniques works well, in an iterative process. Some models are better than others at following a list of tasks too, meaning if you give too many things at once you often see things get dropped. Some tools provide different modes for planning (called "architect" mode in Roo Code just as one example), which can be fantastic for complex needs. You can use that mode to plan the details of what you want to get done, then switch to coding mode to do the work. A lot of these were built with software development in mind, but it does work for book writing tasks too, especially things like reviewing your book for consistency, or running simulations like the various workshops described in this book. These modes are not to be confused with the types of models we are discussing now, thinking models can also do coding for example, they are not fine tuned to do so. The modes provide the model with some additional context to help guide it on a specific type of task.

CODING MODELS

Think of a coding model as an LLM that has been through a rigorous "developer bootcamp." It has been trained on billions of lines of code from public repositories, programming tutorials, and technical documentation. This intensive training makes it not just a text generator, but a powerful AI pair programmer that understands the patterns, syntax, and logic of multiple programming languages.

Core Purpose and Functionality

Coding models are designed to act as assistants across the entire software development lifecycle. Their primary functions include:

- **Code Generation:** Creating functions, classes, or entire scripts from natural language descriptions (e.g., "Write a Python script that scrapes a website and saves the headlines to a CSV file").

- **Code Completion:** Intelligently autocompleting the next line or block of code based on the existing context, often referred to as "boilerplate" code.

- **Debugging and Optimization:** Analyzing a snippet of code, identifying logical errors or bugs, suggesting corrections, and even refactoring code to be more efficient or readable.

- **Code Translation:** Converting a piece of code from one programming language to another (e.g., translating a function from Java to Python).

- **Documentation and Explanation:** Generating comments that explain what a piece of code does or providing high-level documentation for a project.

Key Levers and Prompting Strategies for Coding

Controlling a coding model requires a shift in strategy from creative text generation to ensuring logical correctness and precision.

Temperature (The "Precision Dial"):

- **Description:** This is the most critical parameter for coding. It controls randomness.

- **Impact:** For coding, you almost always want a **very low temperature** (e.g., 0.0 to 0.3). This forces the model to choose the most probable and syntactically correct tokens, leading to functional and predictable code. A high temperature would introduce "creative" but likely buggy and non-working code.

Context is King (The "Project Brief"):

- **Description:** LLMs can only work with the information you provide in their context window. For coding, this is paramount.

- **Impact:** A prompt without context will yield generic code. To get useful, project-specific code, you must provide context like:

    - Relevant existing code snippets.

    - Specific library or framework versions being used.

    - The desired coding style or conventions.

    - Error messages or stack traces for debugging.

Extreme Specificity and Persona (The "Task Assignment"):

- **Description:** Vague prompts lead to vague code. You must be relentlessly specific in your request.

- **Impact:** Instead of "Write a login form," a better prompt is: "Acting as an expert frontend developer, write a secure login form component using React.js and TypeScript. It must include fields for email and password, client-side validation for the email format, and a submit button that is disabled until both fields are valid." This defines the persona, technology stack, and functional requirements.

Example-Based (Few-Shot) Prompting (The "Style Guide"):

- **Description:** Providing the model with a small example of your existing code is the most effective way to make it follow your style.

- **Impact:** If you want the model to generate a new function, first show it another function from the same project. It will learn your variable naming conventions, commenting style, and overall structure, ensuring the new code fits seamlessly.

Chain-of-Thought for Code (The "Whiteboard Session"):

- **Description:** This is a crucial strategy for complex tasks. Before asking for the final code, you instruct the model to first outline its plan.

- **Impact:** Prompt the model to "First, think step-by-step. Outline the functions needed, the logic for each, and how they will interact. Consider potential edge cases. Then, write the code based on that plan." This forces the model to structure its logic before generating code, dramatically reducing errors.

Iterative Refinement (The "Code Review"):

- **Description:** Treat your interaction with the LLM as a conversation. The first output is a first draft, not the final product.

- **Impact:** Use follow-up prompts to refine the code. For example: "This is good, but can you refactor it to be more modular?" or "Add error handling for cases where the API returns a 404 error." This iterative process is key to arriving at production-quality code.

Most authors won't be using a coding model or prompting style, but you might decide to generate your own author website and build out a magnet for potential readers, or any number of other coding tasks. Using these levers and strategies, you transform the LLM from a generic text generator into a specialized, coding partner that can significantly accelerate development speed and improve code quality. However, **Never trust, always verify.** AI generated code should always be reviewed and tested before you utilize it in production (your author website for example).

33

Conclusion: Your Publishing Journey Begins

You have reached the end of this guide, but you are at the very beginning of your publishing journey. We have explored the entire landscape of modern self publishing, from the foundational work of pre-production to the technical details of production and the strategic decisions of distribution. We have demystified the tools, decoded the platforms, and built systems to make the entire process manageable.

But the most important takeaway is not a specific tool or technique, but a philosophy.

Embrace Your Archetype

Are you a **Strategist** or a **Technologist**? Understanding your natural inclination is the key to building a publishing business that doesn't just produce books, but also brings you satisfaction. The successful Strategist who uses powerful, user friendly tools to rapidly publish is just as valid as the successful Technologist who builds a custom, automated "Book as Code" pipeline. Know yourself, and choose the path that aligns with your strengths. Also, it's completely fine to have a hybrid where you mix and match elements from both if that fits your style.

Build Your System

Publishing is not a single, monolithic task; it is a series of interconnected systems. You have a system for writing, a system for editing, a system for production, and a system for marketing. By breaking the process down into these manageable parts, you transform an overwhelming mountain into a series of achievable steps. This book has given you the blueprint for those systems.

Use AI Technology to Level the Playing Field

Artificial Intelligence is the most powerful tool an author has ever had. It is your tireless research assistant, your endlessly patient brainstorming partner, and your 24/7 marketing intern. But as we saw in the final section of this book, the true power lies in moving beyond simple prompts.

The AI powered author doesn't just ask questions, they build their own answers. They create custom assistants using RAG that know their worlds better than anyone. They use AI voice synthesis to open up entirely new revenue streams through audiobooks, a market that was once prohibitively expensive. They transform marketing from a chore into an automated, data driven engine for audience growth.

Mastering this new frontier isn't about learning to code, it's about mastering the conversation. The skill of **prompt engineering** (to provide clear context, assign expert personas, and refine your instructions) is the ultimate lever for turning a general purpose tool into a fantastic creative partner.

The Final Step

You now have the map. You have the tools. You have the systems.

The only thing left to do is the most important one: **Publish your book.**

Take the knowledge you have gained from these pages, choose your path, and take the next step. Your readers are waiting.

www.ingramcontent.com/pod-product-compliance
Lightning Source LLC
Chambersburg PA
CBHW070910130626
46555CB00001B/84